EMBROIDERY
THREADS
AND STORIES

EM·BROI·DER·Y

əm ˈbroid(ə)rē/

NOUN: EMBROIDERY

1.

a: the art or pastime of embroidering cloth

b: cloth decorated with embroidery

"The teams of craftspeople were skilled in embroidery."

Synonyms:

needlework, needlepoint, needlecraft,

sewing, tatting, crewelwork, tapestry

PLURAL NOUN: EMBROIDERIES

2.

elaboration of a story or event

"The story was an embroidery of the era."

Synonyms:

elaboration, embellishment, adornment,

ornamentation, coloring, enhancement

EMBROIDERY THREADS AND STORIES

From Alabama Chanin and The School of Making

NATALIE CHANIN

PHOTOGRAPHY BY Rinne Allen, Sissi Farassat, Robert Rausch, and Abraham Rowe
WITH A FOREWORD BY Rosanne Cash
ILLUSTRATIONS BY Sun Young Park

ABRAMS, NEW YORK

CONTENTS

A FEATHER FINDS A BIRD

NATALIE AND I have a mutual friend, Ann Tenenbaum, and about fifteen years ago, Ann said to me, "You have to meet Natalie Chanin. You two are like the same person." I was already an admirer of Natalie's. I could spend an hour or more at that one little rack devoted to Project Alabama at Barneys New York, in awe and wonder at who made such incredible articles of clothing. They belonged in a museum, I thought. (As I was writing this, I had a sudden longing to see some of the old Project Alabama pieces, went online and saw a T-shirt a woman had "found in the back of her mother's closet" and bought it.)

Ann had some Project Alabama pieces, and she let me borrow a long peach-colored skirt for an event. Again, she said, "You have to meet Natalie. You two are like sisters."

We finally met for the first time in New York, when she was in the city for a trunk sale. She came to my house, and we sat on my little kitchen sofa and talked as if we had known each other for a lifetime.

We talked as if we had been waiting for the other to show up. There was no subject off limits, and it seemed that there was no secret we wouldn't share. Our adventure began.

In 2012, my husband, John, and I took a long trip through the Delta. We started in Greenwood, Mississippi, and visited some of the great geographical touchstones of the South: the grave of Robert Johnson (the Father of the Blues), Dockery Farms and the Tallahatchie Bridge in Mississippi, my father's boyhood home in Arkansas, FAME Studios in Muscle Shoals, and other places that were part of musical lore, part of my own southern history, or places in the South that John and I had dreamed of seeing and soaking up. I had a complicated relationship with the South: There was so much I loved, and so much I felt oppressed by, so much I wanted to embrace, and so much I needed to free myself from. John and I were headed further south on our road trip, to Baton Rouge and New Orleans, but first we went to Florence to see Natalie. We had dinner with her, and the next day we went to the Factory so that Natalie could give me a quick sewing lesson. I wanted to start working on a sewing kit from The School of Making, even though I hadn't embroidered or sewn in decades.

We sat at one of the long tables, and John took out his phone to make a little video of our sewing lesson. Natalie took the needle, threaded it, and then stroked the threads to smooth them out. "You have to love the thread," she said casually. I felt my eyes well with tears. All the questions about my southern heritage, the threads I had to break, the threads I loved or would learn to love— all the questions that had been weighing on my heart, and rumbling in my subconscious, started to surface. Natalie took me to Tom Hendrix's "magic wall" (the Wichahpi Commerative Stone Wall, or Te-lah-nay's Wall), in Florence, and as I sat on the stone bench in the middle of the circle of stones, totems, and sacred objects, I closed my eyes and felt something was meditating *me*, instead of the other way around.

My trip with John continued, and the songs started coming. We wrote a song called "A Feather's Not a Bird," about an urgent journey through the South. I wrote about finding the light inside my own head, about pretty clothes and magic walls, and about learning to "love the thread." The song led to more songs, and became an album, called *The River & the Thread*. It won three GRAMMYs in 2015. The acclaim was wonderful, but more than that, it was a catharsis and a settling of internal rivalries through the power of art, music, and friendship, a deep dive into history, both personal and cultural, and my own way of reckoning with all the threads that have broken, and the strong ones that remain and grow stronger in my own life. It all began with an urgent journey to touch the past, a sewing lesson from a master sister-in-spirit, and an open heart.

ROSANNE CASH

"A Feather's Not a Bird"

BY ROSANNE CASH AND JOHN LEVENTHAL

I'm going down to Florence, gonna wear a pretty dress
Sit atop the magic wall with the voices in my head
Then I'll drive on through to Memphis, past the strongest shoals
And on to Arkansas just to touch the gumbo soul

A feather's not a bird
The rain is not the sea
A stone is not a mountain
But a river runs through me

There's never any highway when you're looking for the past
The land becomes a memory and it happens way too fast
The money's all in Nashville but the light's inside my head
So I'm going down to Florence just to learn to love the thread

A feather's not a bird
The rain is not the sea
A stone is not a mountain but a river runs through me
I burned up seven lives and I used up all my charms
I took the long way home just to end up in your arms
So I'm going down to Florence, now I've got my pretty dress
I'm gonna let the magic wall put the voices in my head

A feather's not a bird
The rain is not the sea
A stone is not a mountain
But a river runs through me

OPPOSITE The Rosanne Coat, New Leaves in Forest Green, couched appliqué and beading, Alabama Chanin

ABOVE Fabric swatch, "A Feather's Not a Bird," reverse appliqué and Stem Stitch embroidery, Rosanne Cash ×
The School of Making collaboration (see more about embroidery stitches on page 129)

ind, the rain...

INTRODUCTION

SOME YEARS AGO, I STOOD ON A STAGE in New York City and believed I was dying. I was supposed to begin telling a story when I felt my head begin to separate from my body—levitating approximately six inches above my shoulders. The guests in the audience of The Moth Mainstage, barely visible under the dimmed floor lights, didn't seem to notice. I'd prepared for this moment for months and now I found myself wondering how many people before me had died standing on this spot. "Are you okay?" the host for the night kindly asked, looking at me and taking my arm. I didn't answer. *Can he not see that my head has detached from my body?* I wondered. He gently turned me toward the microphone and the audience. In the audio recording of this moment, you can hear my voice waver, crack, and then, somehow, begin . . . : "I am from a small town in Northwest Alabama. And in that place, and at the time I grew up, it was about buttoning yourself up, being tucked in, and hiding things away."

So much of my life led to that moment. There was an afternoon in 1994, in Savannah, Georgia, when, out of character, I returned to a quiet house midday, climbed stairs to my third-floor room, turned on the television—which I never did—and landed on a station playing short clips from an NPR *Lost & Found Sound* radio program entitled "Route 66: The Mother Road." Everything I understood about film and documentary work, storytelling, and my ideas of how to look at the world were forever changed that afternoon.

There was a moment standing on the corner of Eighth Avenue and Thirty-Eighth Street in New York City when I knew I must go home to the Alabama of my childhood to look for quilters who knew, and quilted with, my grandmother (see page 64).

OPPOSITE Textile Story Quilt featuring appliqué Rose pattern and the embroidered names of women and family members who knew or quilted with Natalie's grandmother Christine Smith and aunt Mag Rhodes. Materials: ca. 1940s upcycled quilt, organic cotton jersey, reclaimed feed and flour sacks, button craft thread, embroidery floss

There was a road trip that brought me back to my hometown, in the dark of night (see page 73). There was a total eclipse of the sun, where the world went dark. There was a night, lying in the middle of an 'imperial' rose garden, laughing at the sky. There was a wedding in Naples, Italy, dancing. There was a moment, realizing that I was swimming alone with barracuda, in a secluded cove of a tiny island, off the coast of Venezuela. So many moments led to that night standing on the stage at The Moth.

Since that night, I've spent quite a bit of time talking with The Moth's artistic director, Catherine Burns. She is a whip-smart, Alabama-raised soul sister who knows about stories, why they are important, and how to draw them out of people. The famous astronaut Mike Massimino revealed to her that telling his story at The Moth was scarier than his hours-long spacewalk to repair the Hubble Space Telescope as it revolved around the dark side of planet Earth. We talked a lot about the terror of vulnerability, standing before a seated crowd with just a single microphone and stand. But, Catherine insists,

vulnerability and fear and redemption are what connect us as humans. Our stories, should we tell them, all share those dark nights of the soul, but also the clear morning light that rises. I guess I'm in good company, living my life in fear—and despite fear.

In her book *When Things Fall Apart*, the Buddhist nun and teacher Pema Chödrön writes: "So the next time you encounter fear, consider yourself lucky. This is where the courage comes in. Usually, we think that brave people have no fear. The truth is that they are intimate with fear. When I was first married, my husband said I was one of the bravest people he knew. When I asked him why, he said because I was a complete coward but went ahead and did things anyhow."

I am intimate with that mix of cowardice, fear, and bravery.

Toward the end of August 1999, I was on a street corner near my apartment in a northern European city where I'd been living and working as a stylist for almost a decade. As a stylist, I was the person

in charge to organize, make, or otherwise collect the clothing, costumes, and accessories for photo shoots, commercials, films, and all kinds of media. Over this decade, I'd built a business with partners and seen those partnerships end. I'd married a man I loved but was now in the process of separating from. I found myself that afternoon standing in my own neighborhood feeling unsatisfied, unhappy, unsure, unstable, insecure, miserable, and filled with fear. I stood there, frozen. And then I smelled the faintest whiff of snow.

There is a very particular smell that hints of snow. It is a smell that is crisp and solitary. It is the smell of nothing and everything. It smells of ice skates and winter walks, but also of dark days and sunless months. On that late August afternoon, the idea of the impending winter and snow stopped me in my tracks. A thought clearly whispered in the back of my mind: *Winter is almost here, and you won't be here on the other side of it.* In the same moment, I realized that in the warm Alabama home of my childhood, they were picking August tomatoes.

The Alabama tomato that grows in August is perfect. It evokes the color of the deep red soil where it grows; it smells of earth, and verdant green, and home. That day—with the smell of snow in the air—I remembered myself as a girl born of the warmth, a woman who should be eating Alabama tomatoes and not thinking of unpacking winter clothes in August. Even facing a deep fear of life, my past failures, all my future mistakes, and the idea of snow, I sensed this little shimmer of warmth, and of what a different life might look, smell, and feel like.

I knew then that if I wanted to survive, I was going to have to leave. I needed to feel warm again. I remembered a chain of tiny islands off the northern coast of Venezuela called Los Roques.

One of the perks of working as a stylist is that sometimes you are booked for work in beautiful, faraway places. One such occasion was when I worked on a television commercial for a candy bar on the island of Gran Roque in the Los Roques archipelago. It was a dream job, and my first trip to

PREVIOUS LEFT TO RIGHT View from Brooklyn Heights toward Manhattan and the World Trade Center, February 2000; the National Arts Club, New York City, on the night Natalie told her story of coming home for The Moth, 2014; Heirloom-grown Alabama tomatoes, The Factory Café at Alabama Chanin, 2014; Natalie's backyard garden with August tomatoes, 2016, tomato vines "tied up and staked" using Cotton Jersey Ropes (see page 237 in the Techniques and Instructions section)

ABOVE Contact sheets of photos taken during Natalie's sabbatical—from Los Roques and La Gran Sabana, Venezuela, to Brooklyn Heights and New York City

FOLLOWING Fabric swatch, Cadence in Sapphire Blue, reverse appliqué, Alabama Chanin

South America. I'd packed a few bathing suits for an actor and an actress, a sarong or two, a couple of towels, and my styling tool kit and headed off with the film crew to this magical place.

When we arrived, the crew set off scouting locations, getting cameras unpacked, and doing all the things that one needs to do to make a film. Of course, my unpacking and setup took less than an hour. With the few bathing suits and sarongs laid out, I was free to explore the island. That afternoon, I walked footpaths and relaxed for a time on the beach, but soon found myself wandering the island. I wound up at El Canto de la Ballena, a little posada where we were to have our dinner each night. It was owned and run by a woman named Nelly. I found out later that she was famous for her delicious kitchen, elixirs, bar, and the fact that sailors and travelers from around the world gathered around her tables. So, in the first days of that trip, I wound up sitting at one of her tables during the hottest part of the day, helping to peel garlic for the evening meal. I didn't speak a word of Spanish and Nelly and her team didn't speak a word of English, but I loved sitting at that table, peeling garlic until the oils burned my fingers and being lulled by their musical banter. I wound up making two more trips over the next years and fell more and more deeply in love with the place, the water, and the people— and I peeled a lot of garlic.

So that day that I smelled impending winter, I knew that despite fear and obstacles and marriages and partnerships gone wrong, even with the love of friends, and growing children, and a deep, deep sense of my life unraveling, I wanted to go back to Los Roques, Gran Roque, and Nelly's kitchen table. Sure enough, a few months later, I found myself on a small prop plane, making a bumpy landing onto the broken concrete strip that serves as the Los Roques airport. I arrived with a single backpack, a camera, all my past failures, and a future that seemed invisible.

Quickly, I settled into island life, as well as a daily search for myself and my elusive future. I'd rise early each day and hike up a small mountain of volcanic rock that served as the eastern boundary of the archipelago. I'd sit there and watch the sun rise over the expanse of water. Just below, at the end of a sheer drop, was a tiny cove where the force of the ocean had pushed through a kind of chute between the island and a small volcanic outcrop. On stormy days, the water would rush between the island and the outcrop and smash against the cliff, spraying up from the cove all the way to where I was sitting. I came to call it "Angry Cove." In all my months on the island, I never saw a human in that cove or on the tiny pristine beach at its very corner. It seemed only birds thrived in this beautiful but brutal spot. In fact, to get there, you'd have to go by boat or take a rugged hike that traversed the edge of a lagoon— mostly in the water, climbing slippery volcanic rock, shimmying around edges and corners before finally arriving on the tiny sand beach. As my time on the island was coming to an end, I set my mind on visiting that spot I'd watched so often from above.

So, one morning when the weather permitted, I packed a small bag of supplies and headed out. Hours later, I arrived at the small strip of sand, the tiniest beach in the whole world and the gateway to Angry Cove. What first shocked me when I landed on the beach was the sound. The water was so strong that the huge pieces of detached coral were crashing and smashing together in the waves like a symphony. It was so loud and so beautiful.

I stood there completely alone, mesmerized by that singing coral, the ocean, the sky, and the fact that I had made it around the world, around the lagoon, around my life, and I still didn't know where I was going. In so many ways I felt like a failure. I'd ruined a marriage; I'd disappointed my family; I'd left my friends. It seemed that I'd blown up my life. Fear and deep loneliness settled on me. I plopped down on the beach and felt like I'd never move again—never go anywhere. But then I did. I don't know how long I'd been sitting there when the overwhelming urge to swim came over me. I wanted to wash away everything that had come before; perhaps I wanted to wash myself away. It was as if everything in the universe was pushing me into the water, so, despite an internal terror of going into this Angry Cove, I stripped to my bathing suit and walked in. I'm a good swimmer, so I swam through the strong waves toward the middle of the cove where the water settled to a roll, and I lay there floating on my back, spinning, and looking to the sky. It was me, the water, the cliff, and the birds. I floated there for a time, and finally rolled over on my stomach to see what lay beneath me. As I opened my eyes in the water to look down into depths, I realized that I wasn't alone. Below, beside, and all around me swam a giant school of barracuda—it seemed thousands of them. Some of them were almost as long as I was, their sharp teeth visible. I felt like I remembered from some National Geographic special that they could be aggressive. They were like menacing soldiers swimming in formation all around me. Later, I found out that I was in what is known as a barracuda tornado. The silent, circular funnel surrounded me and continued as far down as I could see in the crystal-clear water. In this moment of fear, my failures, my joys, my successes, my aloneness, all circled

me with the barracuda. So, I did the only thing there was to do: breathe, float, and wait through the rising and falling of the waves. Without really knowing it, I suddenly felt sand under my hands. Looking back, I think the barracuda must have taken me as one of them—wild and circling and part of the cove, the Caribbean, the universe. I was connected to their tribe. After my hands felt sand, my feet automatically planted themselves on the beach and it was like I was lifted by something outside of myself. A strange scream erupted from that same center of my body where my aloneness had been. I felt like the sound must have been heard around the world, but the reality was that no one heard a thing. My scream became a part of the singing coral that was pounding in the waves. I was still alone—except, of course, for the barracuda and the birds. I'd been christened that afternoon, by the Angry Cove, by the singing coral, by my own fear, and my loss of fear. That was the day I started my journey back to life. I told myself that I'd never be afraid again. I can't say that I live or have lived every day without fear, but I began to see my life with the same sense of connection and courage I felt standing on that little beach.

That moment was the beginning of Alabama Chanin and The School of Making. Every step I've taken since that day has led me closer to home. Twenty-one years later, I sit here and think that this may not be redemption, but it looks like something that veers in that direction. Creative process is filled with fear and vulnerability, and yet, we rise up every day and keep making stories.

NATALIE CHANIN
July 2021
Florence, Alabama

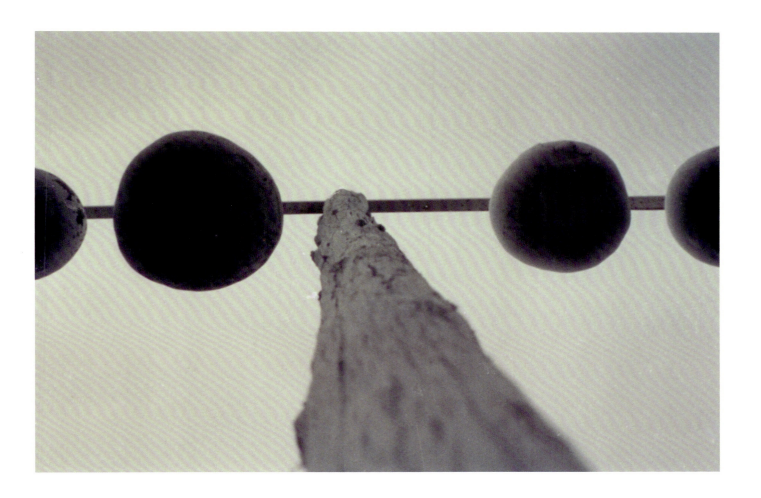

PREVIOUS The Chandler Jacket, Alabama Tweed in Tea, Alabama Chanin, photographed in Athens, Georgia

OPPOSITE Fabric swatch, Tiny Eggs in Doeskin, backstitch quilting, Alabama Chanin—design inspired by photo above

ABOVE Purple Martin Gourds on pole, photographed by Natalie on the road trip from New York to Alabama (see page 73 to read her story of coming home)

CHAPTER 1
CRAFT

THE WORD *CRAFT* is both a noun and a verb. It can describe an activity involving skill in making things by hand, or the action of exercising skill in making something. Add "man" or "woman" to the end of this word and we become *craftswomen* and *craftsmen*, words often used as honorific titles for the most worthy and celebrated makers. Add the letter *y*, and you get *crafty*, which is sometimes understood as homemade or even mischievous. Though the notion of craft is sometimes diminished to the purview of children and quirky creative types, it has traditionally held a significant place in society and thought. Great thinkers, from Plato to Hannah Arendt, have debated *Homo faber*—"Man the Maker"—as the concept that human beings are able to control their fate and environment as a result of the use of tools (craft). Man, woman, and person as maker is man, woman, and person as active participants in the life of the society, the nation, and the world.

This book doesn't resolve the debate of man as thinker vs. man as maker, it isn't a primer for design fundamentals, and you won't learn everything there is to know about choosing colors, making a dress, or designing a collection. It is a story about artisans and makers, of Alabama Chanin and The School of Making, and, in a best-case scenario, it's about finding inspiration, following a path, and, sometimes, about the joy of design. There are ideas about color and how to design a stencil pattern, some basic instructions for sewing stitches, and techniques for embroidery. There are conversations about cotton, and manufacturing, and, perhaps, there is inspiration—although, in my opinion, inspiration is always in the eye of the beholder. There are fabrics and maps for how fabrics are developed. There are people to meet, narratives to paint, and stories to embroider.

OPPOSITE Fabric swatch, Abstract in Sand, backstitch negative reverse appliqué, The School of Making (for more on the Abstract pattern, see chapter 5, beginning on page 160)

CRAFT AS CITIZENSHIP

GROWING UP IN THE RURAL SOUTH, I watched the women in my family shape raw materials, including food and fiber, into life-sustaining products to feed, clothe, and inspire our family. They crafted beautiful lives. Lessons and memories of this time helped shape my enduring vision of living arts and encouraged me to form a life of connection, harmony, and creative pursuit. I followed in the footsteps of these inspiring women as a young mother, photographing my world and using it as a basis for a portfolio that would eventually land me in a Bauhaus-based design program at North Carolina State University.

Since then, I've spent much time thinking about craft, as it eventually became the foundation of my work as a designer, entrepreneur, craftswoman, writer, teacher, artist, and maker. Though these vocations have the internal connection of craft, it has been my experience that in our society there are professional and disciplinary boundaries that can obscure that connection. I've often asked, "What relevance do design, craft, art, and making have in our contemporary society?" I came of age at a time when the United States functioned as a country of makers. We made steel, and textiles, and cars and appliances, and did it so well. American makers designed and produced an array of products that in turn enriched lives, families, and communities. From the rural South and our maker-farms to regional factories, and beyond, *American-made* most often meant well-designed, well-made goods that could last a lifetime—and in some cases, many lifetimes, through the generations of families.

In my own community of Muscle Shoals, in Northwest Alabama, friends and family members grew cotton, which was transformed into knit jersey, and eventually became T-shirts that were shipped around the globe. Fashion trends in the 1950s and '60s turned the simple white T-shirt—once something worn only as an undergarment—into high fashion. In a 2015 article for Vogue.com, Laird Borrelli-Persson praised its plainness and versatility, and the fact that it "leaves room for self-invention, the root of the American dream." A few years later, The Museum of Modern Art highlighted T-shirts as the ultimate sartorial garment (and blank canvas for the wearer's self-expression) in its exhibition *Items: Is Fashion Modern?*

Colored, printed, striped, and embroidered versions of this basic tee became de rigueur for a new generation of fashion icons who used this canvas to establish identity and build groups of like-minded people—immediately recognizable by the declaration printed or stitched on the T-shirt worn. "I am punk." "I belong to this sorority." "I am from this state."

While Muscle Shoals was becoming "The Hit Recording Capital of the World" (see "The Band Tee and Community," page 58), the two-square-mile radius of the Florence-Lauderdale Industrial Park, just across the Tennessee River, was working three shifts around the clock to become the "T-Shirt Capital of the World." While factories containing (*continues on page 49*)

OPPOSITE The Love Tee, Natalie's all-time favorite T-shirt, Alabama Chanin, produced by Building 14 in Florence, Alabama, using organic cotton

FOLLOWING Cotton in the field, Northwest Alabama

In 2012, Alabama Chanin collaborated with designers, farmers, and ginners to grow and harvest organic cotton in Northwest Alabama. This project served as an experiment to reenact a vertical textile system in the region, utilizing organic cotton.

ABOVE FROM LEFT Picking organic cotton by hand; detail of cotton in boll

FOLLOWING PAGES Fabric swatch, Flora in Maize Yellow and Natural, whipstitch appliqué, Alabama Chanin; bales of organic Alabama cotton await processing at Hill Spinning in North Carolina

ABOVE A truck departs the Scruggs & Vaden cotton gin after delivery in Lauderdale County, Alabama, 2012

OPPOSITE At Hill Spinning in North Carolina, cotton moves through various processes of cleaning, carding, and, finally, spinning to make thread. Here, an in-between step reveals fluffy tufts and soft loops of cotton, before the final step of spinning. The mill's owner proclaimed it the cleanest cotton he had ever seen.

FOLLOWING Looking up toward one of the many machines at Hill Spinning that our hand-picked organic cotton ran through on its journey from field to fiber

ABOVE LEFT After being spun into thread, the hand-picked organic cotton is knit in the round into jersey at Professional Knitters in South Carolina. Hundreds of threads of fine cotton are threaded by hand on their machines and then knit together into Alabama Chanin's signature cotton jersey.

ABOVE RIGHT Rolls of organic cotton fabric awaiting shipping

OPPOSITE Embroidered garments from Alabama Chanin collection in the Victoria pattern (see page 206 for a version of this fabric design)

knitting, dyeing, and sewing facilities sprung up in the small industrial park on the edge of Florence, bands from across the globe were crafting and recording music in Muscle Shoals, a short drive away. But still, both textile mills and recording studios were surrounded by farmland, like that of my own family, that both supplied and inspired the growing crafts. This story was, and is, both local and global.

It took me several years to realize that most of the cotton T-shirts I collected as raw materials were most likely made in this community (see "Straight Stitch and Community," page 64). It is a full-circle story: planting seeds, growing cotton, knitting fabric, T-shirts being made, the shirts traveling the world, belonging to individuals as declarations of their tribes, of being worn and loved and discarded and recovered, only to wind up being cut apart and crafted back together again in the very community where they originated. In his important work *The Craftsman*, Richard Sennett writes, "Craftsmanship names an enduring, basic human impulse, the desire to do a job well for its own sake." Any job, any vocation, any calling. He continues, "Craftsmanship cuts a far wider swath than skilled manual labor; it serves the computer programmer, the doctor, and the artist; parenting improves when it is practiced as a skilled craft, as does citizenship." When I think about this idea that craftsmanship cuts a "wider swath than skilled manual labor," I can see the straight line that connects the craft of my professional community of farmers, spinners, knitters, dyers, sewers, designers, and the wearers. This notion of interconnectedness forms the basis of my work. In belonging to a community of makers, I have had the opportunity to learn and practice my craft as well as to become a better citizen.

LEFT Organic cotton fabric on the cutting table in Building 14, the Alabama Chanin manufacturing division.

FOLLOWING Winter morning in North Alabama, after the harvest (see "Alabama," page 73)

GARMENT
AS NARRATIVE

"The thing that stands out the most for me about this work is how the garments are treated as narratives. Like short stories we can all wear. The idea that everything doesn't have to be this huge operation that mass produces quickly. I admire that there was, or is, no rush to relocate to New York or LA but that this part of southern culture could be an export to the world from a small hand-making factory in Alabama."
—MICHI MEKO, *artist and collaborator*

FROM 2005 TO 2006, Michi Meko, an artist and Muscle Shoals native, worked with a range of collection stencils to airbrush graffiti-style patterns onto a selection of garments. These garments were then hand-sewn and embellished in collaboration with a growing number of local artisans.

RIGHT Dropcloth from the production of the Alabama Chanin Collection, featuring the hand-painted botanical-inspired "Florence" stencil

Stenciling, hand-painting, and graffiti-style application of paints are at the core of the lean-method manufacturing process. This hand application of pattern means precious organic cotton jersey is cut and patterns are applied only once a garment has been ordered—reducing waste throughout the manufacturing process. A graffiti-like ghost of patterns is left on the drop cloth and fabric work surface. These fabrics are then upcycled to create new garments and projects. (Read "Stencil Motif Design 101" on page 250 in the Techniques and Instructions section.)

ABOVE Hand-sewn "Graffiti Tee" made from upcycled T-shirts and fabric scraps that are a result of the manufacturing process, Alabama Chanin

OPPOSITE Fabric swatch, Bloomers in Black, reverse appliqué, The School of Making

"The thing that stands out the most for me about this work is how the garments are treated as narratives. Like short stories we can all wear. The idea that everything doesn't have to be this huge operation that mass produces quickly."

—MICHI MEKO, ARTIST AND COLLABORATOR

ALABAMA
CHANIN

MATERIAL 100% Organic Cotton
ITEM 28 58

OPPOSITE Detail of a hand-sewn "Graffiti Tee" showing the Alabama Chanin label

ABOVE Hand-sewn "Graffiti Tee" made from upcycled T-shirts and fabric scraps that are a result of the manufacturing process, featuring Bloomers (see page 189) and Stripe patterns, Alabama Chanin

THE BAND TEE
AND COMMUNITY

WELCOME TO 1969. The Rolling Stones had just landed at the Northwest Alabama Regional Airport to record three of their classic songs—"Wild Horses," "You Gotta Move," and "Brown Sugar"— at Muscle Shoals Sound Studio. Five years before, at FAME Studios, Aretha Franklin had gone there to record what was considered the first big hit of her career, "I Never Loved a Man (The Way I Love You)." The Shoals was gaining national notoriety as a hub for music production. But the region was producing something else too. Across the Tennessee River, just six miles away, cotton was being grown and T-shirts were being made in three shifts a day, destined for band tours, protests, and every wardrobe in America. The Shoals community was bustling with work and sending small parts of itself into the larger world, in the form of these simple cotton garments. In her chapter entitled "Tribes," from *The T-shirt Book*, Charlotte Brunel

OPPOSITE Muscle Shoals Sound Studio

writes that in fashion trends among diverse tribes of people, the T-shirt would carve out "the lion's share for itself." She continues, "New trends in music gave rise to their own gangs, where outfits— in distinctly anti-fashion mode—cast the T-shirt in a major role." The Rolling Stones' "tongue and lips" logo, also known as "Hot Lips"—designed by John Pasche in 1970 and inspired by the Indian goddess Kali—would go on to become one of the most iconic T-shirts ever made and is still produced today. "The graphic tee," Stephanie Kramer writes in *Items: Is Fashion Modern?*, "has come to signify deep-seated memory, identity, experience, and connection for its wearers." T-shirts, ubiquitous, allow individuals and tribes to promote their identities and preferences. For the past six decades, billions of T-shirts have been produced across the globe, emblazoned with everything from favorite restaurants and sports teams to bands and kindergarten classes.

NOTE: *In 2019, we officially folded two decades' worth of research in the material culture of fashion, clothing, and textiles into a nonprofit 501(c)(3) organization we call Project Threadways. (See "Makeshift, Threadways, and Connection," page 215.)*

ABOVE Welcoming travelers to the City of Muscle Shoals, Alabama, "Hit Recording Capital of the World"

OPPOSITE LEFT Organic cotton seedlings

OPPOSITE RIGHT Sewing machine detail in Building 14, the manufacturing arm of Alabama Chanin in Florence, Alabama

CHAPTER 1 CRAFT 61

ABOVE Mick Jagger recording at the Muscle Shoals Sound Studio, photographed by bassist David Hood, 1969; Muscle Shoals Sound Studio T-shirt

OPPOSITE Historic recording booth at Muscle Shoals Sound Studio

STRAIGHT STITCH
AND COMMUNITY

IT'S A HOT AUGUST in the year 2000 and I am standing on the corner of Thirty-Eighth Street and Eighth Avenue in New York City. I've just completed a series of meetings, visiting a few of the multitude of embroidery shops nestled across New York's Garment District. I'm holding one of the cheap plastic I♥NY bags, so ubiquitous at the time, which contains a few samples I have produced from recycled T-shirts purchased from the Eighth Avenue Goodwill store. The cotton shirts have been cut apart and hand-sewn back together again, while sitting on my bed in a tiny rented apartment at the Hotel Chelsea—fifteen blocks away.

I've been showing my hand-embroidered garments to sample room bosses, looking for help in producing the two-hundred-piece project I've envisioned to present at New York Fashion Week in just six months. All of the shops I've visited have turned me down, shaking their heads, and, as I've come to joke over the subsequent years, most likely thinking me a "bag lady." Such are the humble beginnings of my work with cotton jersey, thread, paint, and stitches.

Standing there, feeling defeated, it suddenly occurs to me that since the recycled T-shirts are sewn and embellished with a simple Quilting or Straight Stitch, there are women in my hometown who know how to do this work. In fact, I think, women who had stitched quilts with my own grandmothers are still there, using this simple stitch to create for their friends and community. This is the moment I decide to go home.

RIGHT Fabric swatch, Lee in Earth Brown, reverse appliqué, Alabama Chanin

The Mother of All Stitches

BY FAR THE MOST COMMON stitch utilized in hand-sewing since the Paleolithic era (see page 152), the Straight Stitch is also the easiest and therefore often the first stitch we learn to make as children—as soon as our small fingers are nimble enough to pass a needle in and out of the fabric. Purists call this the "mother of all other stitches." Indeed, all other hand-sewing stitches are created by varying this stitch's length, spacing between stitches, and/or the direction of the stitch. The Straight Stitch has also been called a Running Stitch, as you can "run" several stitches at a time onto your needle; a Quilting Stitch, indicating a tiny version used to bind the layers of a quilt together; and a Basting Stitch, which is simply a longer, more spaced-out version of the Straight Stitch that is traditionally used as a temporary anchor or "pin" to secure fabric in position until a permanent stitch can be applied. Additional embroidery stitches can be created by using all these variations and by adding twists, loops, and patterns. (See page 124, "The Dot and the Line," for more about stitch variations and *The Geometry of Hand-Sewing*— our book dedicated to beloved stitches.)

HOW TO SEW A STRAIGHT STITCH
Bring your needle up at A, go back down at B, and come up at C, making stitches and spaces in between them the same length.

OPPOSITE Fabric swatch, Palm in Wax, reverse appliqué, Alabama Chanin

FOLLOWING Fabric swatch, Stripe in Gilded Black, reverse appliqué, Alabama Chanin

CHAPTER 2

CREATIVE PROCESS

IN MY TWENTY-ONE YEARS of working as the designer and creative director of Alabama Chanin, I've been questioned more about creative process and inspiration than any other single theme or idea. There is a famous story about the poet Ruth Stone catching the end of a poem as it passes through her body and, in that moment, transcribing the poem to paper in reverse order, from the last word to the first. This is a dream creative process, but, unfortunately, not one that I've ever experienced. Creating can be painful and vulnerable, or at least slow, which explains the constant search for "inspiration" or "secret sauce" or perfect setting—anything at all that will simplify and expedite the process. But in my experience, there is no shortcut; however, if I keep showing up, day after day, the work and inspiration arrives. I make a rule with myself that I will show up in fear; I show up in love, and when it rains, and when the sun shines, and when I'd rather be a thousand other places but here. I show up in doubt, and grief, and joy. I show up to do the work—even if the work is one sentence or a single board or a stitch. Showing up is a commitment to something greater than ourselves; showing up is the commitment to ourselves. As Rollo May puts it in *The Courage to Create*, "Commitment is healthiest when it is not without doubt but in spite of doubt."

Doubt doesn't go away with time, but it does go away some days. Either way, we still show up.

OPPOSITE Hand-sewn label detail from the back, Gilded Gold, Alabama Chanin

ALABAMA

THE ORIGIN OF THE WORD *Alabama* is still debated. Some believe it is derived from the Choctaw language, translated as "thicket clearer"— hinting at the agriculturally adept tribes that cleared the thicket for cultivation. As a child, I was certain that this was the best interpretation, as, left untouched, the mesophytic forest of our region produces a landscape so dense and thick with vegetation that it can be difficult to navigate. With an annual rainfall just four inches shy of rainforest designation, the woods and creeks are deep, dark, breathing organisms, filled with plant and animal life, that constitute one of the most biodiverse regions in North America.

Once I'd made the decision to return home to search for the quilters of my childhood (see page 64), this dense vegetation, red clay earth, and the verdant smell of home began to dominate my dreams. Nights dreaming of wooded paths, long gravel roads, and meandering creeks were followed by days and weeks of writing a proposal for the creation and production of a collection of two hundred one-of-a-kind, stitched-by-hand T-shirts. This collection would be accompanied by a twenty-two-minute documentary film, entitled *Stitch*, about old-time quilting circles (see page 82). After raising

money and organizing production of the T-shirts and short film, I called my aunt and explained my big idea, asking if she knew of a house I could rent as a production studio, project headquarters, and living arrangements for a month. A few days later, she called back. She had the perfect place. The future production studio, built by my paternal grandfather in 1958 with, and for, his best friend, sits next-door to my aunt's home—the house of my maternal grandparents—where I had spent much of my youth. I remember holding the phone, astounded at the notion that this project would come to life in my own grandparents' backyard— the place my journey began. In a moment, I saw this work unfurling like an impossible dream, coming to life in unbelievably surprising ways.

That December, I rented a car and drove with a friend, and future business partner, from New York City to Alabama. It was an adventure that crossed eight states and included stops at thrift stores for project materials, dreaming, taking photographs, and visiting with friends and family along the way. Three days and a thousand miles later, we arrived, late in the evening of December 23. As we pulled into the drive, the redbrick house was barely visible, as the future project headquarters had been uninhabited for the previous five years and Mother Nature had begun the process of repossessing the property for her own. My aunt and mother had used a chain saw to cut a path through the dense overgrowth to the back door. Passing through the teeming mass, we made it inside. I was home.

We unloaded the car, which smelled lived-in and was filled to the roof with bags of used T-shirts, and entered the house. It was not an olfactory improvement: the closed-up smell of *(continues on page 80)*

OPPOSITE Field at Mooresville, Limestone County, Alabama, Muscle Shoals National Heritage Area, Hidden Spaces project

ABOVE Piney Creek, Tennessee River backwater, Limestone County, Alabama, Muscle Shoals National Heritage Area, Hidden Spaces project.

OPPOSITE LEFT TO RIGHT Spiral screen print design inspired by *The Dot and the Line* (see page 124); County Road, Limestone County, Alabama, Muscle Shoals National Heritage Area, Hidden Spaces project.

FOLLOWING Fabric swatch, Tony in Ochre, appliqué couching of cotton jersey ropes, Alabama Chanin (see page 237 for how to make cotton jersey ropes)

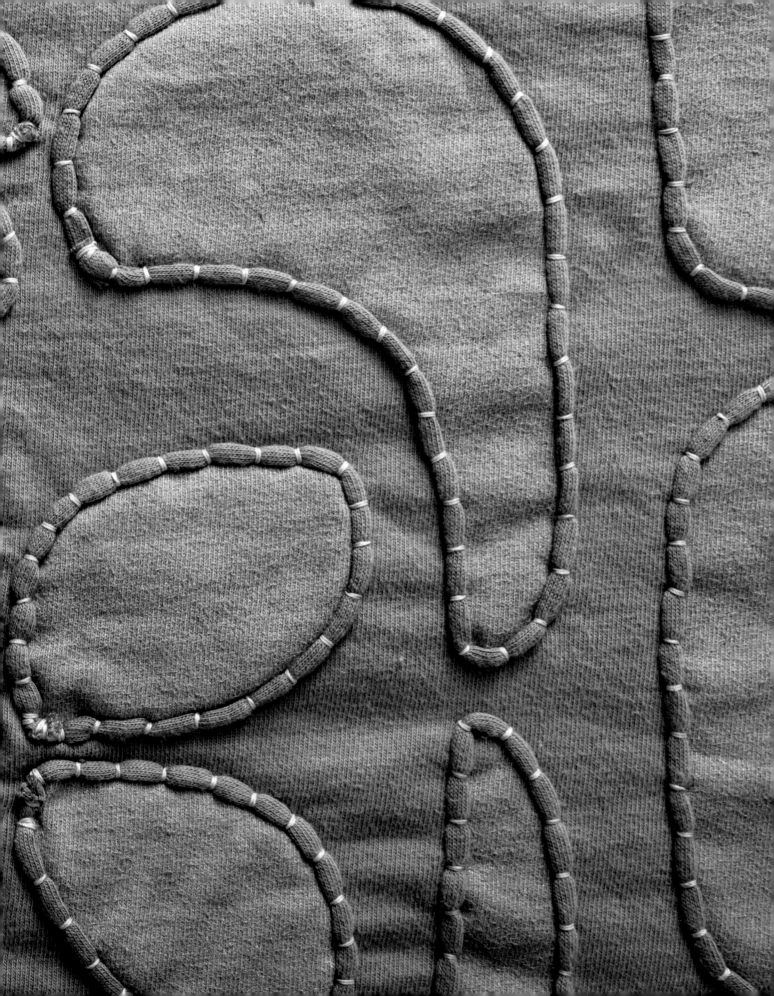

ABOVE Tennessee River at Koger Island, Muscle Shoals National Heritage Area, Hidden Spaces project

OPPOSITE LEFT TO RIGHT Lovelace Crossroads production office; between the fields, Lauderdale County, Alabama

FOLLOWING December sky from the backyard of the Lovelace Crossroads production office, Florence, Alabama

mildew, ghosts of long-ago meals, an odor of unseen animal life, and abandonment. Once settled, I tucked myself, exhausted, into bed, a simple mattress placed on the 1970s vinyl floor of the open main room. Lying there in the dark, perfectly still, I was filled with utter doubt and dread. My mind racing, I dissected my life and its decisions: running away from this place, working, living, loving; experiencing accomplishments and failures, adventures, successes, and losses. I started to cry and couldn't stop. I felt my entire life culminating in this dark night of the soul, waiting for ghosts and unknown creatures and bitter cold to seep through the cracks and crevices of floorboards, walls, and windows black with night. Throughout those hours of darkness, my senses remained highly tuned for sounds and smells, for the snakes that were most certainly coming to join me in the warmed bed as soon as I closed my eyes. Finally, in the very early morning light, I fell asleep only to awake with a start from dreams of snakes and living, moving topiaries. Despite my fear, I was greeted by a beautiful, clear day; there were no snakes or ghosts to be found.

December light in Alabama is crisp and bright, the sky a remarkable color of winter blue. On this Christmas Eve morning, the first in the brick house at Lovelace Crossroads on County Road 200, I got up and went to the kitchen, cleaned a small place on the counter, and made my morning tea. Sitting down on one of the stools that my aunt had sweetly left for us, I looked around the room and took stock. In addition to the vinyl flooring, I noticed the walls of the room were covered with an old, broad-board paneling. I stood, wondering what the years-long coating of life and abandonment hid underneath. I cleaned one board, discovering a beautiful pine board. This paneling—historically prevalent across the region—was designed to mimic paneling originally cut from the magnificent southern longleaf pine, the Alabama State Tree, whose ancient forests across the state were called "Giants of the South."

Reclaimed, I found the one board spectacularly beautiful. Inspired, I cleaned one more, and then another. Board by board, I worked my way around the entire room throughout the day. As the sun began to set outside the kitchen window, I sat back down on the stool, drinking in the room, the light, and the pine boards. In reclaiming them, I realized that I had also reclaimed something of myself, my history, my home, my family, and my life.

I then remembered the Rollo May quote and understood anew that commitment and creativity and life are healthiest when they are not "*without* doubt but *in spite* of doubt." Watching the sun slip down behind the thicket, I remember thinking, yet with the presence of doubt, "I can do this."

STITCH:
THE FILM

IN THE SAME MOMENT I dreamed of making the first T-shirt collection, I also envisioned a short documentary film about why and how people made quilts. I'd been working in the film industry for almost a decade and had been dabbling in documentaries. I imagined interviewing my grandmother and other ladies like her, who had learned quilting from their own mothers and grandmothers. The stories of old-time quilting circles felt like a deep and inextricable part of the T-shirts I was holding. *Stitch* was to become that film.

A couple of weeks after I had arrived in Alabama, but while I was still cleaning boards and setting up our "home headquarters," two friends from Vienna, Austria, turned up to work on filming part of the project. Sissi, Jakob, and I planned to crisscross three counties in an old blue Chevy truck my father had donated, to capture stories on video and 8mm film. I was excited to connect with groups of quilters who, I'd also hoped, might help sew the shirts.

We began filming at the Central Community Center, a concrete block building located four miles north of the brick house at Lovelace Crossroads. The Community Center sat just beside the volunteer fire department for the incorporated town of Central, Alabama—ten miles from downtown Florence. It was often used for family reunions, luncheons, fundraisers, and community gatherings. And for quilting. A group of women—sisters, neighbors, and friends—had formed a quilting circle that met every Tuesday in a back room. There, they took in quilt tops and joined together the top, batting, and backing layer of the quilt with tiny neat Quilting or Straight Stitches (see page 67). They donated all of the proceeds from their quilting back to the center. Seeing their familiar faces, listening to talk of their lives and stories of my grandparents, and witnessing their work was a joy. We filmed them sitting around the quilt that was "put up" on the quilting frame, laughing and talking, working, telling stories, and enjoying the fellowship of one another.

I excitedly told them about the project, both the film and the collection, and our plans to present during New York Fashion Week. After much laughter and many stories, they politely let me know that they weren't interested in sewing T-shirts for Fashion Week. They loved me but didn't care about fashion. It sounded like the "work of

OPPOSITE Early hand-stitched T-shirts were cut from existing cotton jersey garments gathered from across the region and beyond. This design, called the "Sister Shirt," utilized three different recycled T-shirts to complete the pattern.

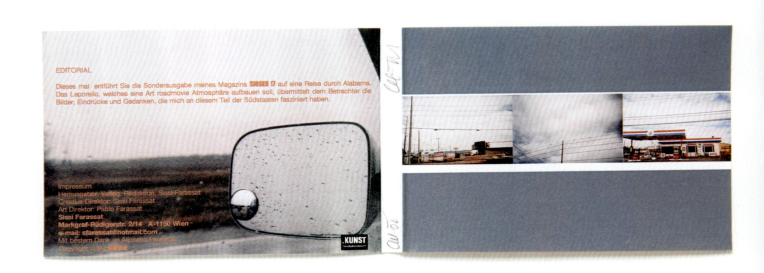

ABOVE AND OPPOSITE Booklet spreads from *Sioseh 17: Alabama*, Sissi Farassat, photographed across three counties of Northwest Alabama during the filming of *Stitch*, 2000

The camera operator and cinematographer (and my dear friend) Sissi Farassat has become a world-renowned artist—who does amazing stitching on her own photographs. The photographs above are from her archive of this trip. Not a single person involved in the making of this film got paid. The digital versions of both the four-minute trailer and the twenty-two-minute documentary are available to watch on the Alabama Chanin journal (see Sources and Further Reading on page 226 for more information).

FOLLOWING The original *Stitch* VHS cassette that played at the Hotel Chelsea, 2000

younger people," they said, describing their lives and retirement, their kids and grandkids, common acquaintances, their churches, their homes, and the work of winter gardens.

In the course of our month on the road, we often visited my own grandmother and filmed her talking about her memories of making and sleeping under quilts—and of seeing her mother and grandmothers making these beautiful heirlooms. With cameras and microphones in hand, we interviewed quilters and people from across the community about their memories of quilts and quilting circles.

A trailer for the film played at the Hotel Chelsea on VHS tape as the first collection of two hundred one-of-a-kind T-shirts was presented. The twenty-two-minute documentary was completed that spring and shown in galleries and stores and where the shirts were sold. The final film was a result of thirty-five hours of digital interviews with approximately thirty people, four rolls of Super 8 film, 469 miles in that blue pickup truck we called "Old Blue," one prop plane, and a crew of three who rambled around (and above) Lauderdale, Limestone, and Colbert counties in Northwest Alabama with the deepest curiosity. (Photos from all three counties can be seen in the section titled "Alabama" on pages 72–81.)

Watching the trailer and the film two decades later, it's clear that a key part of my journey home, the success of Alabama Chanin, and the invention of The School of Making had to do with this group of friends and neighbors, now spread across the globe and the heavens. Many of the ladies and gentlemen who told their stories in the documentary have since passed away, including my grandmother. I feel incredibly lucky that I

got to hear and document a small part of their histories—and their way of life. Every single one of our interviewees said, "Things were different back then; it's not like it is today." How true that statement rings, and I wonder how it will be viewed in twenty more years. Looking back, I see that this was the beginning of Project Threadways (see page 215) and the desire to record the stories of textile workers across our region and nation.

REVERSE APPLIQUÉ AS INVENTION

EARLY IN MY T-shirt-making adventure, before going home, an acquaintance approached me about producing a small run of shirts for an online store she was planning to open. After months of hand-sewing T-shirts, I was excited about the opportunity and scoured flea markets and suppliers in the greater New York City area to find perfect vintage T-shirts to work on and appliqués to machine-sew onto these pieces. The final agreed-upon design used a vintage raglan T-shirt with a combination of numbers and letters, finished with iron-on Swarovski crystals. I made samples and then worked with suppliers to secure the needed components. However, when it came time to produce the shirts, one of the suppliers failed to deliver some of the appliqués. Frustrated and without options, I began to brainstorm how I could avoid this in the future and apply letters and numbers to T-shirts without being tied to unreliable suppliers.

During a morning of creative exploration, I had a vision: a number was stenciled on the T-shirt with a second piece of fabric stitched behind, and this backing-layer revealed by cutting away the inside of the stitching line on the outer T-shirt layer. My very first reverse appliqué T-shirt was stenciled with spray paint from the hardware store down the street, sewn by machine—with help from the tailor working at the dry cleaner across the way—and cut out to reveal the backing-layer with a less-than-perfect pair of scissors. In the next weeks, I began sewing stenciled shapes by hand using the Straight Stitch (see page 67), with Button Craft Thread (see page 159), and a perfect pair of embroidery scissors (see pages 239–241 for more on scissors). And thus, reverse appliqué was "invented."

Of course, I didn't invent reverse appliqué that day at the Hotel Chelsea; this method of layering different colors of fabric and exposing desired layers through cutting and stitching had been done across centuries and cultures. In creative flow that day, I had experienced what is known as *cryptomnesia*, or the act of a forgotten memory being remembered and, through the remembering, believed to be a new and original thought. I had forgotten, remembered, and believed deeply in this new and inventive process of reverse appliqué.

This simple act of remembering and arriving back where I started changed everything for me. After being home for some time, I finally understood that memory sometimes collaborates with the universe to reverse one's own course in life; we can go back; we can look underneath, and, in the same moment, we can both uncover and create newness.

OPPOSITE One of the earliest T-shirts produced for the "Alabama" collection featuring the purchased vintage raglan T-shirt, appliqués, and Swarovski crystals. This design, and the complications of production, would eventually lead to hand-sewn reverse appliqué being introduced into the collection.

REVERSE APPLIQUE

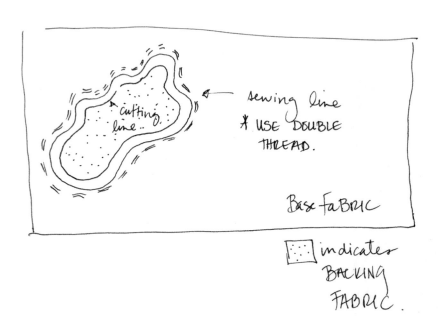

cutting line

sewing line
* USE DOUBLE THREAD.

Base FABRIC

▢ indicates BACKING FABRIC.

- PLACE BACKING FABRIC BEHIND AREA to BE APPLIQUED and PIN to SECURE.

- STITCH AROUND EVERY SHAPE <u>INDIVIDUALLY</u>, MAKING SURE to TIE OFF PROPERLY. THIS METHOD HELPS SHIRT RETAIN ITS STRETCH. (ESPECIALLY at CHEST!)

- SEPARATE FRONT and BACK and <u>CAREFULLY</u> CLIP FRONT <u>INSIDE</u> <u>SHAPE</u>.

- TRIM INSIDE, MAKING SURE NOT TO CUT TOO CLOSE TO SEAM

Reverse Appliqué

Reverse appliqué became the basis for all that Alabama Chanin and The School of Making are today. It is the first technique artisans and guests to our studio learn; it is the core of our entire stable of techniques. The simple number stencils grew to include roosters, and eagles, and flowers. These stencils were inspired by rural life, the community, historic textiles, cutting-edge fabric design, and more. Using these, reverse appliqué T-shirts were created, produced, shipped to stores around the globe, and photographed by major fashion magazines as our cottage-industry-inspired business model garnered attention from journalists, culture writers, and entrepreneurs. Over time, the simple stencils and stitches of these first T-shirts developed into elaborate designs that used an array of stenciling, hand-painting, threads, yarns, materials, and techniques in multiple layers that required detailed fabric maps to be replicated by artisans whose skills grew in lockstep as the designs evolved—all inspired by basic reverse appliqué.

MATERIALS

Stencil or design for project

Textile paint, marker, or other method to transfer stencil or design onto project

T-shirt or fabric for top layer of project

Backing fabric that is slightly larger than your stencil or design

Pins

Needles (see page 152)

Button Craft Thread (see page 159)

Embroidery scissors (see page 240)

1   Using a stencil with paint or textile marker, apply your design to the right side of your T-shirt or top-layer fabric, and let the design dry thoroughly. Follow any manufacturer instructions for setting materials permanently.

2   Place the backing fabric, right side up, behind the stenciled area of the top-layer fabric to be appliquéd, and pin into place.

3   Using a Straight Stitch (see page 67), stitch the two layers of fabric together along the edge of each design or stencil shape, beginning and ending each shape with a double knot.

4   Using sharp embroidery scissors, clip a small hole in the top layer and inside your stitched shape, being careful to only clip the top layer of fabric. Insert the tip of your embroidery scissors and carefully trim away the inside of the shape, cutting about ⅛" to ¼" (3 to 6 mm) away from the stitched outline.

OPPOSITE Handwritten and -drawn instructions for reverse appliqué from the original "Stitch Book," used in the production of the early hand-sewn T-shirts.

PREVIOUS The Bloomers pattern (see page 189) was one of the first all-over repeating patterns incorporated into early designs. This fabric swatch shows a Washed Black over Black organic cotton, hand-embroidered using the reverse appliqué technique to highlight the repeating leaf pattern (see Techniques on pages 230–231 for more on hand-embroideries).

OPPOSITE Contact sheet of photos from the production studio at Lovelace Crossroads.

ABOVE Natalie holding a Wrap Shirt using the Bloomers pattern (see page 189), hand-embroidered using the reverse appliqué technique as part of an early collection, Lovelace Crossroads, 2002

THE FAMILY
OF STITCHES

pile held between their hands, he would say, "Now, break it." When the bundle proved impossible to break, he would deliver his point: "This is family; can't be broken."

THERE IS A LEGEND in my family about a lesson my grandfather Perkins, who was called "Perk," told to every child when he felt they had reached an age of understanding. He would take each child, on their own, into his front yard on the side of the county road known as "Mud Road," instructing them, "Pick up all the sticks you can find and bring them back here to the steps." He would sit on the steps watching, eyes shining, as a child-sized armload of small sticks was gathered. Once the sticks were deposited on the stoop, he would place one small stick in the child's hand and say, "See if you can break this." Of course, because a single stick is not strong, each of the children could easily break it. Perk would respond, "This stick is you on your own, fragile and breakable." Then he would counter, "Now I want you to take as many sticks as you can hold in your two hands." Once the child had gathered the sticks into a neat

My grandfather's story, and the physics behind the process, inspired the larger stitches we use at Alabama Chanin and The School of Making. T-shirts, at their core, are simply a knitted web of cotton jersey created by making tiny interlocking loops with a small, fine yarn. Sewn with Button Craft Thread (see page 159) and the small quilting stitches I'd learned as a child, my first shirts fell apart. After puzzling over the problem, I realized that, like the bundle of sticks, a family of stitches and loops were needed to carry the weight of my heavier, more robust thread. Thus, long stitches and double knots became a key part of the design and making process.

In making with fabric and thread, we needed a family of stitches. The same is true in work and life. We need a family—colleagues, friends, heroes, heroines, inspirers, and mentors—stitched with us to carry the weight. Perk taught me that.

OPPOSITE Fabric swatch, Alabama Fur in Natural, Alabama Chanin; Small backstitches with embroidery floss leave exposed knots to create the Alabama Fur fabric that is still a staple of the Alabama Chanin collection.

ABOVE "White Room 2," Hand-embroidered photograph by Sissi Farassat, 2020

OPPOSITE Hand-embroidered Pencil Skirt using the Alabama Fur technique and the Tony pattern

FOLLOWING Fabric swatch, Tony in Black, Peacock Blue, and Ochre, three-layer reverse appliqué
(see chapter 6, beginning on page 176, for more on stencil designs and the Tony pattern)

CHAPTER 3
FLOW

THE TENNESSEE RIVER cuts a path right through the center of The Shoals—splitting Florence from the cities of Muscle Shoals, Sheffield, and Tuscumbia. Before the construction of Wilson Dam as part of the National Defense Act of 1916, the river flowed wide and shallow, and was prone to flooding and rife with shoals. Muscle Shoals is named after one of these shallow shoals. Heading downstream, boats and rafts had to be carried with "muscle" over or around the obstacle. Below the shoals, the river became narrower and deeper, and thus, navigable by boat. For this reason, by the 1890s, textile mills were moved to the region, brick by brick, and the river was used to transport cotton and finished goods that were the products of a vertical system where cotton was grown, ginned, spun, knit, cut, and sewn. With the completion of Wilson Dam, electricity produced by the river was used to run machines and power the factories that were transforming fiber to garment.

The textile history of this region can be attributed, for better or for worse, to this river flowing right through its center. Eventually, of course, the North American Free Trade Agreement (NAFTA) would help to carry this industry away—as, machine by machine, it flowed to the next location.

OPPOSITE Late afternoon shadows over a bend of Colbert Creek; numerous creeks and tributaries join the Tennessee River channel as it winds to the Ohio River and on to the Mississippi River, eventually meeting the Gulf of Mexico

ABOVE Vintage map of the Tennessee River Valley at the Shoals from Natalie's family home. Wilson Dam on the Tennessee River was completed in 1925 and generated power for the many textile plants that would settle in this region.

OPPOSITE Electric Tower pattern for screen print in collaboration with Studio Job, an Atwerp-based design studio

FOLLOWING The Tennessee River cuts a path right through the center of the Shoals community in Northwest Alabama; bordering the banks of the Tennessee River are the cities of Florence, Muscle Shoals, Sheffield, and Tuscumbia.

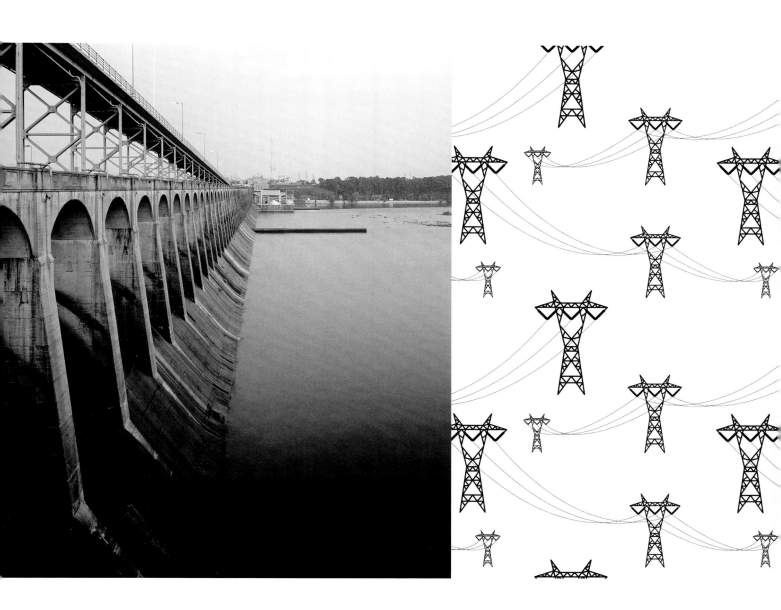

DECONSTRUCT

sewing and quilting." From this tiny printed text, a talented group of twenty artisans was assembled. In symbiotic relationship, we produced the T-shirt collection, stitch by stitch: I, cutting and assembling project packages containing garment pieces, appliqués, threads, and flosses, which the artisans turned into finished goods with embroidery stitches.

When the T-shirts were finished, a small handmade catalog was produced and sent out to press and buyers across the industry. The completed collection was shipped back to the Hotel Chelsea apartment/ showroom, and a music-video-style trailer for *Stitch* was produced and played via VHS cassette during Fashion Week (see page 82).

THE PSYCHOLOGIST Mihály Csíkszentmihályi coined the term "flow" to describe an age-old mental state of being fully immersed in a task. Flow is the feeling of being so completely focused on a singular task that time melts away and feelings of joy and satisfaction emerge. And so those first days at Lovelace Crossroads unfolded. The time between arriving at the house at Lovelace Crossroads and showing a finished collection of T-shirts back at the Hotel Chelsea in New York City is a blurry, difficult-to-reconstruct trajectory of moments and days that unfolded across seven short weeks.

Between uncovering the beautiful pine boards, setting up the house and studio, and preparing for the filming of *Stitch*, I began to cut apart T-shirts, explore embroidery stitches, and interview artisans. I ran a small classified advertisement in the local paper that read: "Part-time hand-

Through a twist of fate—and a story I heard many years later—one of the first calls we received was from Julie Gilhart, then the Fashion Director of Barneys New York. Julie reviewed the collection herself, then sent the buyers from Barneys back a few days later. The buyers made their selection and placed an order for "twelve embroidered like this and twelve colored like that and twelve similar to these" in a range of sizes and colors. I reminded everyone, "These are one-of-a-kind shirts, collected across eight states." Looking at one of my favorite shirts, printed with "Smith Family Reunion, Roanoke, Virginia," the buyers replied, "Just make something comparable in a similar color." As the week progressed, my friend, and soon-to-be partner, received orders from eight of the most prestigious stores in the world, a small article ran in *Women's Wear Daily*, and I was headed back to the house at Lovelace Crossroads to begin the process of turning a one-off embroidery project into a business.

OPPOSITE "Customizing," lines applied to T-shirt indicate a variety of customized styles that can be created by deconstructing the garment in different ways, special project, 2016

OPPOSITE Fabric swatch, String Quilting in Camel, organic cotton scraps.

ABOVE Cover to an early "Alabama" catalog featuring a stitched-down, printed photograph taken by Natalie looking out the back door of the production office at Lovelace Crossroads, designed by Subtitle NY, 2001

ABOVE Alabama Collection T-shirt, Lace in Bleached Brown, beaded reverse appliqué, recycled cotton T-shirts, 2000

OPPOSITE "Alabama" catalog featuring a color photocopied detail of a Lace patterned T-shirt in Bleached Brown, recycled cotton T-shirt, 2001

ABOVE "Alabama" catalog featuring a color photocopied detail of the Eagle patterned T-shirt, reverse appliqué, recycled cotton T-shirts, 2001

OPPOSITE Re-creation of an Alabama Collection T-shirt, Eagle in Navy and Alabama Red, reverse appliqué, recycled cotton T-shirts, 2021

ABOVE Hand-sewn T-shirts drying on the clothesline at the Lovelace Crossroads design and production studio, Alabama Collection

OPPOSITE "Alabama" rubber stamp for labels, designed by Subtitle NY, 2000

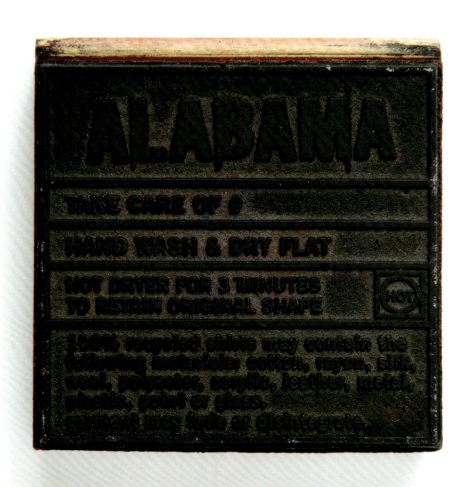

ALABAMA

TAKE CARE OF #

HAND WASH & DRY FLAT

HOT DRYER FOR 3 MINUTES
TO RETAIN ORIGINAL SHAPE

HOT

100% recycled shirts may contain the
following materials: cotton, rayon, silk,
wool, polyester, acrylic, leather, metal,
plastic, paint or glass.
Apparel may fade or disintegrate.

COMMUNITY

MY MORNINGS WERE SPENT cutting shirts apart, packing project kits in the afternoon, and meeting with our artisans in between. At night I ran the washing machine, did the accounting, and prepared for the next day. Weekends were spent shopping for more vintage T-shirts to be used as raw materials. Over four months, the orders were produced and delivered. Soon after, the phone began ringing with news that the stores wanted to see the next season's designs.

As I came to know all our artisans, I learned firsthand about the effects of NAFTA on the ever-dwindling textile industry in the region. The stories of factories and families were beautiful and devastating in equal measure. And as the work evolved, I understood that we were creating not just collections, but also a model for how to design and grow a fashion business in a sustainable way. In a world of fast fashion, mass production, and machines, I wanted to work slowly and thoughtfully; I wanted to contribute to my community. (Learn more about oral histories and Project Threadways on page 215.)

RIGHT Fabric swatch, Florence in Concrete, Black, and Silver, hand-painted, Alabama Chanin. Hand-painted fabrics like the Florence design became another way to utilize recourses and craftspeople from our community. The stories of fabrics like these have been documented through fabric libraries and oral histories collected across two decades.

RANDOM THREAD WORK

- USES RANDOM STITCHES TO FILL IN A SHAPE

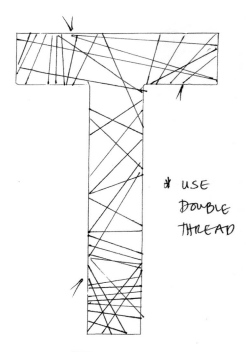

※ USE DOUBLE THREAD

- may also use embroidery stitches, beading or thread embroidery with this Technique

STUDIO BOOK SERIES,
WIRED MAGAZINE, AND
THE SCHOOL OF MAKING

WHEN I WAS FIRST approached about publishing a book on our hand-sewing techniques, I naively responded, "It's already written." I was thinking about a three-ring binder I had compiled of hand-written and -drawn instructions for techniques simply marked "Stitch Book." The collection of pages included all the core techniques we were using for garments and was updated regularly as new ideas emerged—which helped our production team stay on track. The pages included instructions like Double Stitch and Beading (page 123), Reverse Appliqué (page 90), and Random Thread Work (at left).

Turning these instructions into a book, I worked at night, after the studio had closed and the office was quiet, design and accounting duties complete, and vintage T-shirts for the next day's production were washing in the basement laundry facility.

On one of these nights, in November 2004, I sat down with the new issue of *WIRED* magazine. The now infamous issue contained a copy of *The WIRED CD*, subtitled "{Rip. Sample. Mash. Share.}," a music collaboration between sixteen artists and groups and *WIRED*, produced under the Creative Commons License.

It occurred to me while reading this issue that sewing techniques, like music, the culinary arts, and most creative fields, were historical processes, passed down from generation to generation. Each consequent generation riffs and samples and tweaks the works that came before. While we all are products of our own specific generational culture, we are also products of millennia of creative process. In this way, while some suggested that I had invented reverse appliqué, the technique had, in fact, been used since humans took to needle and thread. This realization inspired me to not only write a book on our techniques, but also to share two of our best-selling patterns. I thought, *Take the patterns, take the techniques, and rip, sample, mash, and share for personal use.*

OPPOSITE Handwritten and -drawn instructions for the original "Stitch Book," used in the production of the earliest hand-sewn T-shirts, which became the Studio Book Series (see pages 260-261 for more on these books)

My reasoning behind this open-source idea was multifold:

1   I did not invent reverse appliqué; I had simply accomplished a variation on the traditional version with an unusual material and way of working.

2   Companies much larger than my own were copying the work already, knocking off our patterns and screen-printing stitch lines on garments rather than working with local artisans to complete the laborious process with needle and thread.

3   On a message board on the (then newly expanding) internet, I had read a message about how my work was extremely "elitist" based on pricing. Of course, the writer of this post never considered the artisan work behind the collection, the use of recycled materials, and the extremely hands-on production required to produce a collection of this magnitude.

4   After the three years of work using these techniques, it was clear that these were techniques that were not being taught to consequent generations and that there was an idea of cultural sustainability that should be documented.

5   My hand-drawn stitch book would have a real cover, real illustrations, and a life outside of the three-ring binder.

Many friends and colleagues in the industry warned against moving forward with this book. "You'll be putting the nail into your own coffin," someone commented. The consensus was that once the techniques were shared, no one would want to buy our collection. So, it was with trepidation that I looked toward the publication date of *Alabama Stitch Book* in the spring of 2008.

What happened surprised me. As readers began to experiment with the techniques themselves, they valued them even more. I got messages like, "Oh, now I understand why your garments are worth so much," and "It's very time consuming and complicated to work with recycled materials." Although our Straight Stitches (page 67) are simple, the work takes time to do well. Readers began to experiment and wrote to me about their newfound understanding of the complexity of the embroidery. End of career predictions unfounded, more and more people came to value the work of Alabama Chanin and the generations that came before.

After *Alabama Stitch Book* published, three more books followed over the next four years. This series of four books, what we now call the Alabama Studio Series (page 260), served as the foundation for what was to become The School of Making in July 2014.

Find more in the Techniques and Instructions section beginning on page 228.

OPPOSITE Handwritten and -drawn instructions for the original "Stitch Book": top row, instructions for Double Stitch; bottom row, instructions for Beading

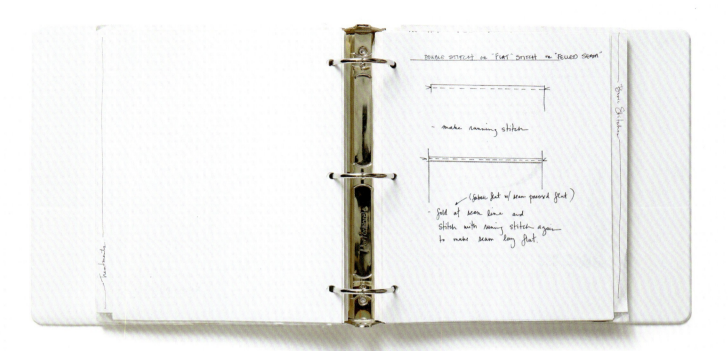

DOUBLE STITCH or "FLAT" STITCH or "FELLED SEAM"

- make running stitch

(fabric flat w/ seam pressed flat)
- fold at seam line and
stitch with running stitch again
to make seam lay flat.

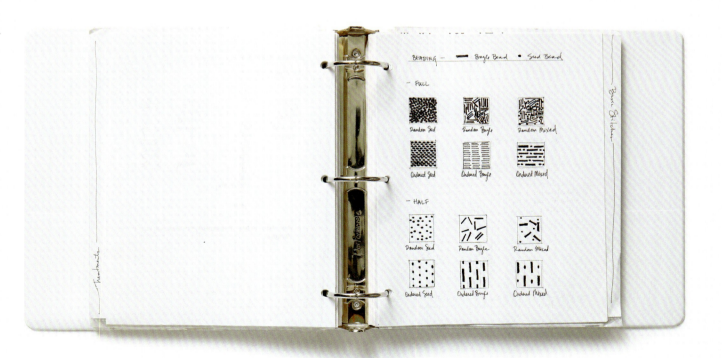

BEADING — — Bugle Bead • Seed Bead

- FULL

Random Seed   Random Bugle   Random Mixed

Ordered Seed   Ordered Bugle   Ordered Mixed

- HALF

Random Seed   Random Bugle   Random Mixed

Ordered Seed   Ordered Bugle   Ordered Mixed

THE DOT AND THE LINE

IN 1972, a few years after the Rolling Stones recorded across the river in Muscle Shoals, my mother, a brilliant mathematician and lover of geometry, introduced me to the book *The Dot and the Line: A Romance in Lower Mathematics*, by Norton Juster. It remains one of my all-time favorite children's books. Juster dedicated *The Dot and the Line* to Euclid, whose books, written around 300 BCE, became the basis for the geometry we learn as children, how dots and lines interact to form the shapes that create our world. After years of teaching embroidery stitches in workshops with The School of Making, it occurred to me that every stitch could be broken down into geometric systems using combinations of points and parallel lines to create a multitude of patterns for threads.

When I moved back home, I had no idea how embroidery stitches would become such a defining part of my work. In 2015, I started writing my favorite of all our books, *The Geometry of Hand-Sewing: A Romance in Stitches and Embroidery*. It was a new way of looking at embroidery based on my love for geometry. The idea was to organize embroidery stitches into a series of grids—based on geometric structure, reducing all stiches to simple repeating dots across parallel lines.

RIGHT Spirograph pattern design for screen printing, inspired by *The Dot and the Line*.

ABOVE Fabric swatch, "Natalie's Dream," Facets in Dove and Faded Dots, embroidery, whip stitch appliqué, and beading, Alabama Chanin

CRETAN STITCH

Cretan Stitch (also called Open Cretan Stitch, Persian Stitch, Quill Stitch, and even Long-Armed Feather Stitch) is a popular stitch for necklines and armholes at The School of Making and Alabama Chanin. Work from opposite sides of the grid structure, sewing towards the center.

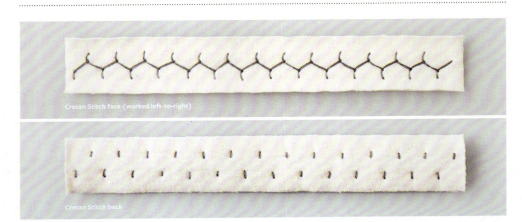

Left-to-right | Right-to-left

● Bring needle up at A, go down at B, and come back up at C, making downward vertical stitch and bringing needle over thread. Insert needle at D and come back up at E, making upward vertical stitch while bringing needle over thread. Continue pattern to end of row.

Cretan Stitch face (worked left-to-right)

Cretan Stitch back

EMBROIDERY STITCHES

The Geometry of Hand-Sewing includes two physical Stitching Cards, which are used as templates for equidistant stitch grids. Cretan Stitch—one of my favorite stitches—can be seen on these pages using this method. See page 260 for more on *The Geometry of Hand-Sewing* and the Alabama Studio Books series.

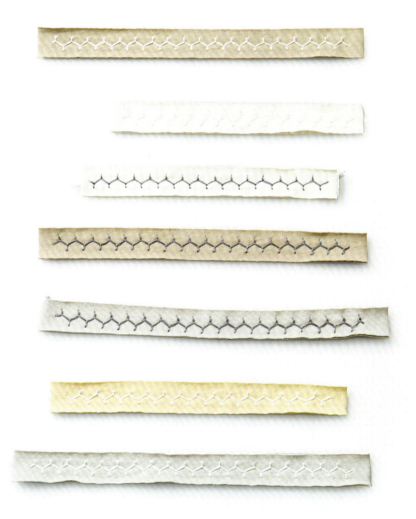

OPPOSITE Cretan Stitch instructions from *The Geometry of Hand-Sewing*, published in 2017

ABOVE Cretan stitch sample swatches

FOLLOWING Fabric swatch, Variegated Stripe in Black and White, appliqué and various embroidery stitches, from *The Geometry of Hand-Sewing*, The School of Making

CHAPTER 4

MATERIALS AND TOOLS

"Most of our lives we live closed up in ourselves, with a longing not to be alone, to include others in that life that is invisible and intangible. To make it visible and tangible, we need light and material, any material. And any material can take on the burden of what had been brewing in our consciousness or subconsciousness, in our awareness or in our dreams."
—ANNI ALBERS

THE BAUHAUS, FOUNDED IN 1919 by German architect Walter Gropius (1883–1969), had as its core objective a radical concept: to reimagine the material world to reflect the unity of all the arts. There was a distinct emphasis on materials and minimalism. Craft and technology played equal roles—foreshadowing the complicated relationship between these two seemingly diametrically opposed concepts today. The reigning principles of the Bauhaus were unity of form and function, the idea that design is in service to the community, and a belief in the perfection and efficiency of geometry.

My degree in environmental design from North Carolina State University, inspired by the principles of Bauhaus philosophy, was not based on the environmentalism we think of as sustainable design today, but on the Bauhaus idea that the entire environment matters. Of course, this is how we should all be thinking about environmentalism.

OPPOSITE The Polo Coat in Navy with reverse appliqué stripes of upcycled fabric scraps, Alabama Chanin, 2020

ABOVE Anni Albers card weaving at Black Mountain College, an avant-garde institution for the living arts where Albers taught Weaving and Textile Design, photograph courtesy of the Western Regional Archives, State Archives of North Carolina, and the Josef and Anni Albers Foundation

OPPOSITE Fabric swatch, Horizon Line in Navy, stenciled, design inspired by textile artist Anni Albers. Anni Albers's quote is from her statement "Material as Metaphor" for the panel "The Art/Craft Connection: Grass Roots or Glass Houses" at the College Art Association's annual meeting. New York, February 25, 1982.

"Most of our lives we live closed up in ourselves, with a longing not to be alone, to include others in that life that is invisible and intangible. To make it visible and tangible, we need light and material, any material."

—ANNI ALBERS

OPPOSITE Fabric swatch, Frida's Dress in Black, appliqué, reverse appliqué, embroidery, and beading, Alabama Chanin. ABOVE Josef and Anni Albers's living room, photograph courtesy of the Western Regional Archives, State Archives of North Carolina, and the Josef and Anni Albers Foundation. FOLLOWING Fabric swatch, Lee in Black, Earth Brown, and Brown Cotton and Indigo Chambray, appliqué and embroidery, Alabama Chanin

COTTON, TOOLS, AND PHYSICS

AS THE PROJECT OF reproducing T-shirts changed from project to business, I settled into life and work in rural Alabama. It was a time of great change in the world as the internet began to find serious traction and dial-up connections were available via phone lines across the country—connecting rural to urban. Concerns about the physical distance between my company and the fashion capitals of the world eased once it became clear that we would not be held back by our ability (or inability) to communicate with companies and decisionmakers anywhere. The very first "internet stores" were beginning to emerge, which helped us acquire materials that weren't readily available locally. Online shipping systems with increased delivery options allowed us to send boxes of garments around the globe, to stores, stylists, and magazines like *Vogue*, *i-D*, and *Spin*. Accounting systems moved to new software and *WIRED* magazine wrote about the "art of coding" as *handwork*—a word aligned more with craft than science. It seemed the Bauhaus ideal to "reimagine the material world to reflect the unity of all the arts" was upon us. The merger of craft and technology— as in my Bauhaus-inspired design training—was visibly and physically at the core of the work we

were doing as a team each day. New methods of communication were emerging and improving at rapid rates, essentially democratizing access to what once seemed out of reach. The iMac and iBook became the devices we used to power the business. The iPod was released in October 2001 and provided the soundtrack to the craft and technology that was unfolding in our brick house at Lovelace Crossroads. The use of scientific development for practical purposes seemed to connect craft and science every day in our working lives.

So as the work with our artisans continued to grow and thrive, I was collecting stories of old wives' tales around the process of sewing during the day and reading *WIRED* magazine by night. I used problem-solving skills learned in design school to think about ways to build a craft-based business through streamlining and updating processes. As I began to connect all the dots, it occurred to me that many of the sewing lessons we were learning from our elders find proof in the functions of physics.

Physics is generally described as the branch of science that orders the structure of matter and how the fundamental parts of the universe interact. While the connections between cotton, the act of sewing, and physics may not be immediately evident, materials (like cotton) and tools (like sewing implements) are parts of the universe that interact in very specific ways to create particular outcomes—in our case, creating garments. Take the simple needle (see page 152), around since the Paleolithic era: Threading a needle has proved to be such a difficult task that many different versions of needle threaders have been invented over the years to simplify the process. Yet there are four rules, first learned as old wives' tales but based on the physics of materials and manufacturing process, that simplify this act.

OPPOSITE Natalie's original iPod, containing soundtracks from past runway shows and events, still functioning and often playing at the design studio today. PAGES 144-145 Fabric swatch, Lee in Concrete Brown and Black, reverse appliqué, Alabama Chanin

OLD WIVES' TALE #1

The end you cut is the end you knot. This saying urges us to thread the needle using the end of the thread coming from the spool and to knot the end with the freshest cut.

FUNCTIONAL PHYSICS

1 **Nap**

Take a spool of thread and hold the end of the thread with two fingers. With two fingers of the other hand, run the finger pads from the cut end of the thread toward the spool and you will feel that it is smooth. This is the nap of the thread. Now run the finger pads from the spool toward the cut end of the thread. You will feel that it is more rough and less smooth. This is going against the nap. Always thread your needle with the nap—from the cut end of the thread back toward the spool. Thread your needle before cutting the thread and use a sharp scissor at a forty-five-degree angle.

When sewing with a single strand of thread, a thread being sewn (primarily) with the nap of the thread tends to have fewer knots and it frays less.

2 **Point**

The twisting method used to manufacture thread creates a direction as the thread is wound onto the spool. The end of the thread coming from the spool is what spinners call the "good end," as the fibers tend to hold a point when viewed under a microscope. The fibers on the other end of the cut thread tend to splay, making it harder to thread this end of the thread with the needle.

OLD WIVES' TALE #2

Needle your thread, don't thread your needle. This saying urges you to move the needle rather than the thread when threading.

FUNCTIONAL PHYSICS

1 **Material Stability**

Needles are made from metal; thread is made from fiber. Metal is stronger than fiber and therefore more stable.

2 **Path of Least Resistance**

If you are right-handed, hold the cut end of the thread between your index finger and thumb of your left hand—about ⅛" from the cut end and with the arm resting on a solid surface. With the right hand, move the needle down over the thread, "needling" the pointed end. The more stable element—the needle—makes this a simpler task.If you are left-handed, reverse this process.

OLD WIVES' TALE #3

Don't lick. This saying urges us to avoid wetting the thread.

FUNCTIONAL PHYSICS

1   **Expansion**
Cotton, wool, and most fibers at their core absorb liquid. When a fiber absorbs liquid, it expands. Licking the thread before attempting to thread the needle can cause the thread to expand, complicating the threading process.

Natalie's Disclaimer: *When working with multiple strands of embroidery floss, it is sometimes necessary to get the strands to "stick" together during the needle-threading process. This idea of licking the thread most likely comes from use of this multi-strand material or thread that was poorly plied, causing the individual strands to splay.*

OLD WIVES' TALE #4

Long thread, lazy girl. This saying urges us to use a thread length that matches the size of our individual forearm.

FUNCTIONAL PHYSICS

1   **Motion**
While it may seem faster and easier to sew with a long thread, the physics of the process shows it is faster to sew with a thread that is matched to the size of your own forearm. If you use an extremely long thread, you spend more time pulling the thread through the fabric than actually sewing stitches. A thread paired to your arm is the perfect size for making stitches and pulling through without stopping.

Determine the length of your thread by holding the end between thumb and forefinger and measuring to the tip of your elbow. Double this length and cut.

2   **Less Is More**
A short thread will knot and tangle less during the sewing process. Excess thread from a longer strand has the tendency to tangle upon itself, causing the sewer to stop and untangle often. Keeping the thread as short as possible, and your working area free of obstructions, will aid in the sewing process.

3   **Friction and Abrasion**
The point of contact where thread meets fabric is under extreme abrasion during the sewing process. Naturally, the thread closest to the needle becomes weaker with every stitch.

PINS AND NEEDLES

ALTHOUGH I'VE ALWAYS FOUND the view from above breathtaking and inspiring, I've never been a particularly calm or comfortable flier. Something about moving 500-plus miles per hour, at approximately 36,000 feet above the earth, and under someone else's command makes me nervous. My chest constricts at every single takeoff, my heart races during the bumpy stretches, and I sit on pins and needles at every landing—never settled until the wheels are connected once again to Mother Earth. A long time before I became a million-miler, I learned that if I could find an inspiring distraction during the flight, my chest would relax, and I could (at least somewhat) enjoy the journey. Hand-sewing eventually became the perfect distraction, as each methodical stitch kept my mind focused and my hands active. It was simple enough that I could stop to enjoy the window seat and small enough to pack away easily, and it could be accomplished in the tight space of ever-shrinking airline seats. I became an even more nervous and distraught flier after September 11, 2001. As rules for what could be carried into airports and onto airplanes changed forever, my need for calming distraction grew exponentially.

In late 2001, while packing for a design trip, I realized that I required a travel tool kit that passed easily through the newly formed Transportation Security Administration (TSA) stations set up at every airport. A small scrap of fabric, my "needle roll" (pictured on the following pages) was this invention of necessity. The pocket-sized roll, cut from leftover scrap fabric, a tiny pair of scissors (see page 233), and a compact sewing bag fit neatly in my carry-on. (Find instructions for the Needle Roll and Travel Kit Bag beginning on page 232.)

RIGHT Mother Earth from above, taken on Natalie's phone

FOLLOWING After travel restrictions limited scissors on flights, Natalie created the Needle Roll, which became an essential for sewing while traveling.

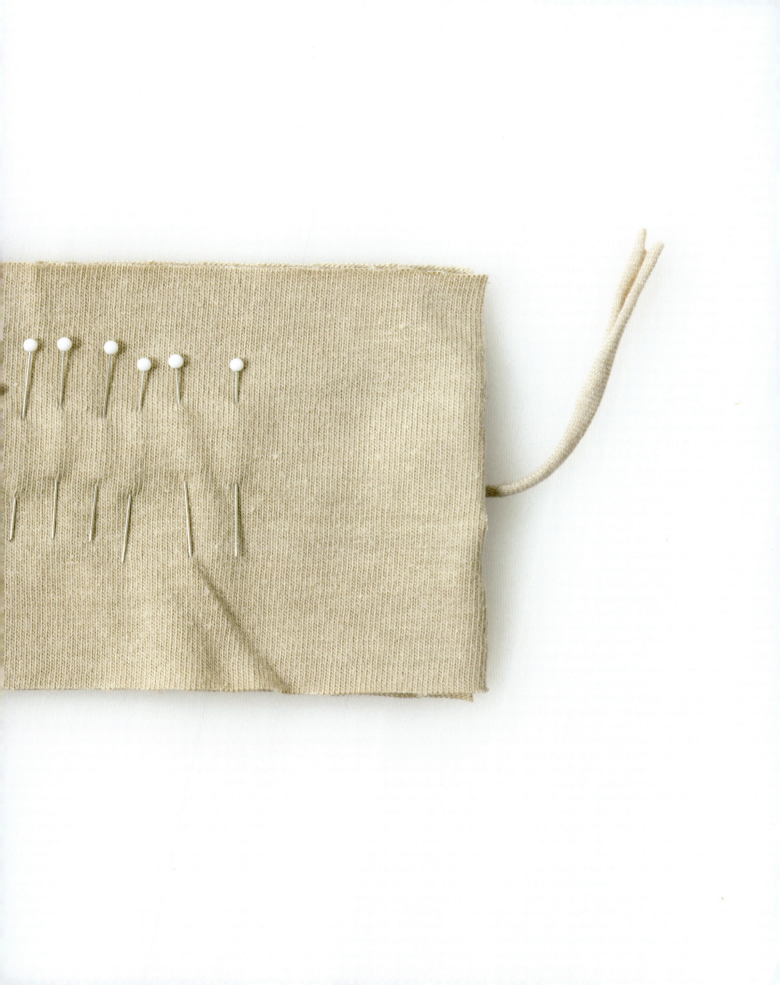

FINDING THE GRAINLINE

COTTON JERSEY, like all fabrics, has a face, a back, and a grainline. In a knit fabric, the term *grainline* refers to the direction of the stitches making up the fabric, which typically run vertically along the fabric's length. Looking closely at the cotton jersey "face," or "right" side, there are straight vertical columns of knit stitches that make up the grainline—in knitting, this is called the "knit side." On the "back," or "wrong," side, there are a series of small loops that in knitting are called the "purl side."

> To cut the fabric with the grain, align your cutting tool with the vertical column of stitches on the fabric face.
>
> To fold fabric with the grain, fold it *along* the vertical column of stitches.
>
> To fold fabric against the grain, fold it *across* the column of stitches.

While cotton jersey does stretch in both directions, it has the most stretch across the grain, hence almost all garments made with cotton jersey will call for the grain to run vertical with the body—from head to toe.

At Alabama Chanin and The School of Making, we apply patterns with stencils to the face of the fabric. (See chapter 6, beginning on page 176, for more on stencils and stencilling.)

RIGHT Fabric swatch showing grainline running left to right, Magdalena in Ochre, stenciled, The School of Making

A BRIEF HISTORY OF NEEDLES

THE #9 SHARP HAS BEEN a favorite needle since that fateful day at the local hardware store (see page 159) and has evolved over many years as one of a variety of different needles for a specific range of designs and stitches. As I became a more accomplished sewer, I began working with a range of milliner's needles—originally designed for hat-making. Although they are prevalent and easy to obtain today, needles were once crucial survival tools that helped change the path of civilization.

Early Paleolithic needles, fashioned from bones, tusks, and antlers, allowed humans to stitch together furs and hides for warmth as they settled in colder regions. The earliest needles had no eye but rather a notch or ridge where sinew or fiber was held and pulled through the material. Archaeologists continue to discover ancient needles in Russia, Turkey, Iraq, Greece, and Britain. In the Americas, native people were beginning to innovate their own needle technology using porcupine quills and parts of the agave plant.

Metal needles came along sometime around the third century BCE, with evidence of iron needles in Germany. Ancient Egyptians were creating their own needle variations from bronze, copper, and silver—and people began to use different types of needles for different tasks. China began working with steel needles and the practice spread to Greece and Rome. Early versions of thimbles and evidence of advanced sewing technology have been found in Roman excavations.

Evidence suggests that metal needle production was truly advanced and perfected in eleventh-century Spain by Muslims who were transforming medical techniques and wanted standardized needles for suturing. When they were driven from Spain, they took their needle-making practices with them, spreading the needle form into Arab nations and across Europe. During the seventeenth century, Europe further developed the technology, handcrafting needles by cutting two needles from a single piece of bent steel wire. By the mid-1600s, Redditch, England, began to work its way to the forefront of needle manufacturing, bolstered by its easy access to waterpower. By 1700, Redditch had approximately six hundred needle-making artisans who were creating the highest-quality, most affordable needles in the world. The first mechanized needle-making processes began in the mid-1800s, and by the 1860s, England was manufacturing one hundred million needles per year.

OPPOSITE AND FOLLOWING Native American sewing needles and awls from the Florence Indian Mound and Museum found in the region surrounding the Shoals.

Needle-making machines were introduced in 1870, but prior to that, all needle "pointing" or sharpening was done by hand. Pointing was the most dangerous job in the factory, yet also one of the most prized, due to the high rate of pay. These workers held unfinished needles to a grindstone and metal slivers could fly up and blind the pointer. The sharpening stones could also shatter, causing terrible wounds or fatal injuries. Inhaling metal dust resulted in a prevalent lung disease called pointer's rot, which was much like coal miners' black lung disease. This illness was so prevalent during this era that the life expectancy of the average pointer was no more than thirty-five years.

As textiles became more beautiful and sought after, and as disposable incomes grew, households had more and more needles on hand. Trade routes expanded and textile fabrics, notions, and tools evolved into valuable commodities. By the 1900s, more than three million needles were produced each day worldwide—with three hundred million purchased each year in the United States.

Although there are millions of needles in the world, it doesn't mean that all needles are equal. I know many sewers and artisans who sharpen and use the same needle for years. Needles have helped grow our societies and cultures, advance our industries and economies, and have allowed us to express ourselves creatively; they are both practical tools and instruments of beauty.

NEEDLE GUIDE

IT IS IMPORTANT TO CHOOSE the right needle for the right job. Consider needles like writing implements: Change the size of the pen tip and a signature will look different; switch to a pencil and the look and feel of the signature will be different again. The same is true of a needle: Change a needle size and/or style and the quality of the stitches can change.

Following are descriptions of a few needles and specific uses. I have found that particular needles work well for particular stitches. Also, the same style of needle from different manufacturers may have different specifications. It's important to try out a variety of styles to find your favorites. For example, the #6 Milliner—designed for use in hat-making—has become my favorite needle for working Straight Stitch (page 67); however, I find a #9 Sharp is better for stitches with small details, like Cretan (page 128) and some looping stitches. Once you find a needle that fits your hand, your embroidery style, and a function, store those favorites in an organized manner, as they can be your tools of choice for years to come. (Find the Needle Roll instructions on page 232.) Test a variety of needles on a scrap of fabric before beginning any project to determine the right needle for the desired outcome.

SHARPS
Sharps are multipurpose needles and have a sharp point with a small, rounded eye, just large enough to accommodate thread. These are the most popular and versatile needles used for hand sewing. Sizes range from 1 to 10.

MILLINER NEEDLES
These needles are long, with round or oval eyes, and are traditionally used in hat-making. They are also used for pleating and smocking. Sizes range from 1 to 11.

EMBROIDERY (CREWEL) NEEDLES
Embroidery needles are similar to Sharps (see below), but have a long oval eye, which makes threading easier when using multiple strands of thread, embroidery floss, or yarns. Sizes range from 1 to 12, with the most popular sizes in the 7, 8, and 9 range.

OPTIONAL: BEADING NEEDLES
Standard beading needles are very fine and long, with long eyes. These needles are suitable to use with beads, pearls, and sequins. Short beading needles are ideal when attaching beads to fabric featuring additional embroidery. We've had success in using a #10 Milliner for beading with our Button Craft Thread (on the following pages). Sizes range from 10 to 15.

OPPOSITE Sewing needles from The School of Making; different types of needles can be used for different stitches and purposes. From top: row 1: sharps; row 2: milliners; row 3: embroidery

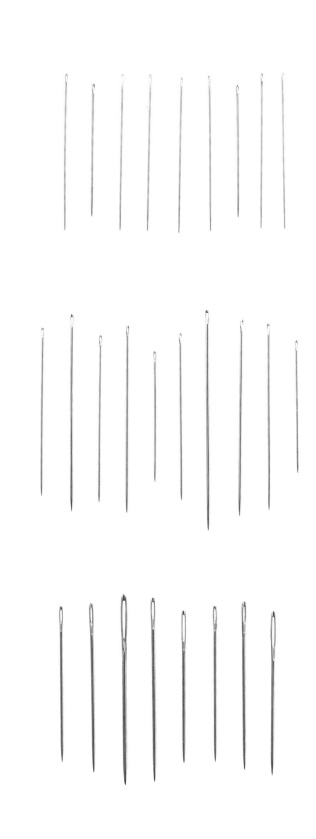

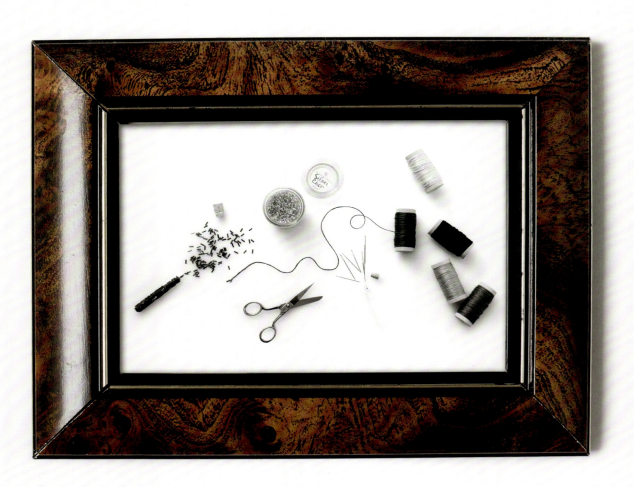

FOR THE LOVE OF HARDWARE STORES

IN THE EARLY AUGHTS in New York City, you could find a hardware store every few blocks. These stores, many that had been there for generations, were neighborhood centers, selling every kind of item a household might require, from tools and nails to washing powder, needles, thread, and pans for cooking. This is where I bought my first needles and spools of thread to begin hand-sewing T-shirts.

After a first round of experiments, I found that the all-purpose thread I was using—designed for machine sewing—was fragile and broke easily after wearing and washing. As I began to sew more and more shirts, I would visit the store almost daily and noticed a heavier-weight thread designed for sewing buttons and crafts, Button Craft Thread, and, although the thread came in only a handful of colors, I bought several spools and headed home. However, when I started to sew, I found that the thicker thread wouldn't fit through the needles I owned.

Back at the hardware store, open spool of thread in hand, I found a package of #9 Sharp needles that had an eye that was wide enough to allow the thicker thread and felt good in my hand. I doubled the thread to give a stronger seam and began sewing the shirts with this new needle and thread. The process worked well, the seams felt strong, and I thought I'd solved the problem. Yet after I'd sewn, worn, and washed the new shirts multiple times, I realized that my small stitches with a double strand of the heavier thread were pulling through the lighter cotton jersey T-shirts and creating holes. Pondering the issue and looking for creative solutions, it occurred to me that if I was going to use the stronger thread, I needed to lengthen my stitches to allow more fabric to support the weight of the heavier thread and knots (see "The Family of Stitches" on page 97). This is when I began the ⅛″ to ¼″ rule for stitch length and started using the larger knots and tails that have become part of the signature style at Alabama Chanin and The School of Making.

While this signature style creates a particular aesthetic, it is also an engineering design that keeps the finished work sturdy and durable. Today, we continue to use the same Button Craft Thread I bought at that neighborhood hardware store, as I've found this thread to be the most durable, abrasion resistant, and easy to use of all the threads we've tested over the years. It is a cotton-covered polyester thread and, although it is only available in a limited range of colors, I believe it is the most durable and viable thread on the market for this way of sewing.

OPPOSITE Beads, embroidery floss, needles, and scissors from The School of Making (see more on materials, tools, and scissors in the Techniques and Instructions section beginning on page 228)

CHAPTER 5

PRACTICE

IN THE 1660S, renowned scientist Sir Isaac Newton completed a series of experiments that led him to a remarkable discovery. In *Opticks*, Newton details how this work with prisms revealed that an object's surface reflects some colors and absorbs others. Later, it came to be understood that the frequencies of these reflected wavelengths are perceived through the human eye. The eye then activates light receptors that transmit information to the brain—which we understand, through language and cultural learning, as color. Thus, color vision is an action occurring between the object, frequency of reflected wavelength, light receptors in the eye, and the brain. But color is also understood and processed culturally. Names of colors and shades are language specific, and colors denote different meanings in different cultural contexts. For example, the cultural construct that pink is for girls and blue for boys is a relatively new and geographically limited construction.

Like seeing color, mixing color likewise involves a physical process. In mixing, pigments are gathered to create paints, inks, and dyes, followed by the chemical process of mixing materials into the compounds that artists and designers apply to surfaces. At the Harvard Art Museum, the Forbes Pigment Collection houses samples of minerals, soils, insects, stones, and other substances that have been used to create pigments. The museum has assembled and documented more than 2,700 pigment varieties and is the largest collection of historical pigments in the world.

OPPOSITE A Navy-colored organic cotton jersey over the Camel color produces a contrasting fabric that emphasizes the Abstract pattern backstitch negative reverse appliqué, The School of Making (find instructions for Experimenting with Color in the Techniques and Instructions section beginning on page 228).

Indeed, for millennia, libraries across the globe have housed troves of volumes in a multitude of languages on color: color as science, color in the natural world, color samples, and books on how to mix, match, name, describe, and organize colors. There are treatises on color from thinkers as diverse as Leon Battista Alberti, Leonardo da Vinci, Sir Isaac Newton, Johannes Itten, and Josef Albers. Published in 1814, Abraham Gottlob Werner's *Nomenclature of Colours* was used by artists and naturalists who were looking to standardize the names and descriptions. The slim volume was famously carried by Charles Darwin on his voyage on the HMS *Beagle* to describe in detail the biological and zoological colors he encountered while traveling the world.

While study of color is a complex and scientific endeavor, the act of seeing color and perceiving a specific hue or shade can be more ephemeral, personal, and cultural. I'm a believer in both science *and* an openhearted, emotional, and subjective experience of color. For me, looking at color is more than the physical act of eye connecting to brain; it involves a squinting of the eyes, a tilting of the head, a changing of the light, a lifting of the chin, and an opening of the senses to feel and define for myself. In *Interaction of Color*, Josef Albers wrote, "In order to use color effectively it is necessary to recognize that color deceives continually."

Find instructions for Experimenting with Color in the Techniques and Instructions section on page 228.

All of the fabric swatches in this chapter are color explorations with the Alabama Chanin, Medium Weight, Organic Cotton Jersey using the Abstract Stencil (see more about the Abstract Stencil in chapter 6: Repeat, beginning on page 176).

PREVIOUS Fabric swatch, Abstract in Ballet and White, backstitch negative reverse appliqué, The School of Making; Textile paint color test swatches on a Concrete-colored fabric in the Abstract pattern

OPPOSITE Tonal fabric swatch has a Camel-colored outer layer with a matching backing layer that produces a subtle pattern, Abstract, reverse appliqué, The School of Making.

COLOR

DUE TO AN OVERWHELMING RESPONSE from stores and the press, one collection of T-shirts became two, two became three, and the work expanded to include T-shirts, skirts, dresses, jackets, and coats—some garments requiring up to twenty-eight recycled T-shirts. As orders grew, the production studio and number of artisans grew in lockstep. It soon became clear that we would require a much larger supply of vintage and recycled T-shirts. We gathered these shirts—many of them originally made from cotton grown a few miles from Lovelace Crossroads—from thrift stores and sorting centers across the country. Then, after being received in the basement at Lovelace Crossroads, these collected raw materials were sorted into piles of similar colors—yellow, red, blue, green, brown, black, and white. In some cases, lights and darks of individual colors were sorted into even more refined piles using a dye book I created in design school as a reference. These sorted T-shirts were then overdyed to achieve a more unified appearance or to create another color altogether. This overdye process "smoothed out" the differences in the original hues and created beautiful variations that were similar but retained a rich nuance. These piles of color, wildly inspiring, would be stacked together in similar hues and tones to await their final design.

From these stacks, the fabric was "harvested," and the T-shirts cut into sections so that garment pattern pieces could be applied, traced, and removed. To these cut garment pieces, color and texture was added from an array of ingredients like inks, textile paints, threads, flosses, yarns, beads, and appliqués. These rich layers of color were added, subtracted, embroidered, manipulated, and embroidered again, finally constructed by our artisans into finished garments. Applied in combination with our stencil designs, there were seemingly limitless opportunities for exploration and creativity.

In some cases, those original recycled T-shirts had been dyed and overdyed up to five or six times, giving them unique patinas. As the company grew and we transitioned into working with rolls of organic cotton jersey, we selected favorite scraps of fabric from the overdyed T-shirts as examples of how we wanted our newly knit fabric colors to look and feel. Seasonal color cards were made for the twice-yearly collections. Twenty-one years later, the influence of this early work in sorting and dyeing remains a beloved piece of our ongoing design aesthetic—one part forever inspiring the next.

Our color cards followed in a long tradition of documenting color and process. We drew continual inspiration from writers, scientists, artists, and designers throughout history. And although we used our basic understanding of the science of color, most of the work with color was a function of learning the science of fabric dyeing and, through practice, ultimately discovering what felt right for a specific collection. Today, I still find that decisions on color are made based on how a particular shade relates to a theme, what emotion a tone might evoke, or, simply, what colors feel harmonious to me as a designer when embroidered and placed together. A single photograph has inspired an entire collection of colors. There are collections where colors have been inspired by the hue of one leaf, and those that are meticulously planned out with gouache painted on paper and fabric ordered to match. There is no given process; rather, there is exploration, inspiration, and finally, using what is in front of us to evolve future exploration and inspiration.

OPPOSITE Fabric swatch, Abstract in Camel and Navy—the opposite layering of color from the fabric swatch on page 161, where the Navy is the outer layer and the Camel is the backing layer, backstitch negative reverse appliqué, The School of Making

OPPOSITE AND ABOVE A repeating Abstract pattern (page 191) can be used for any garment or project. Shown here in a tone-on-tone Peacock layering. The Asymmetrical Trench above was created from a repeating Abstract stencil pattern using backstitch reverse appliqué for The School of Making. A detail of the backstitch reverse appliqué, The School of Making (see Reverse Appliqué on page 91).

FOLLOWING Fabric swatch, Abstract in Navy and Peacock, backstitch negative reverse appliqué, The School of Making

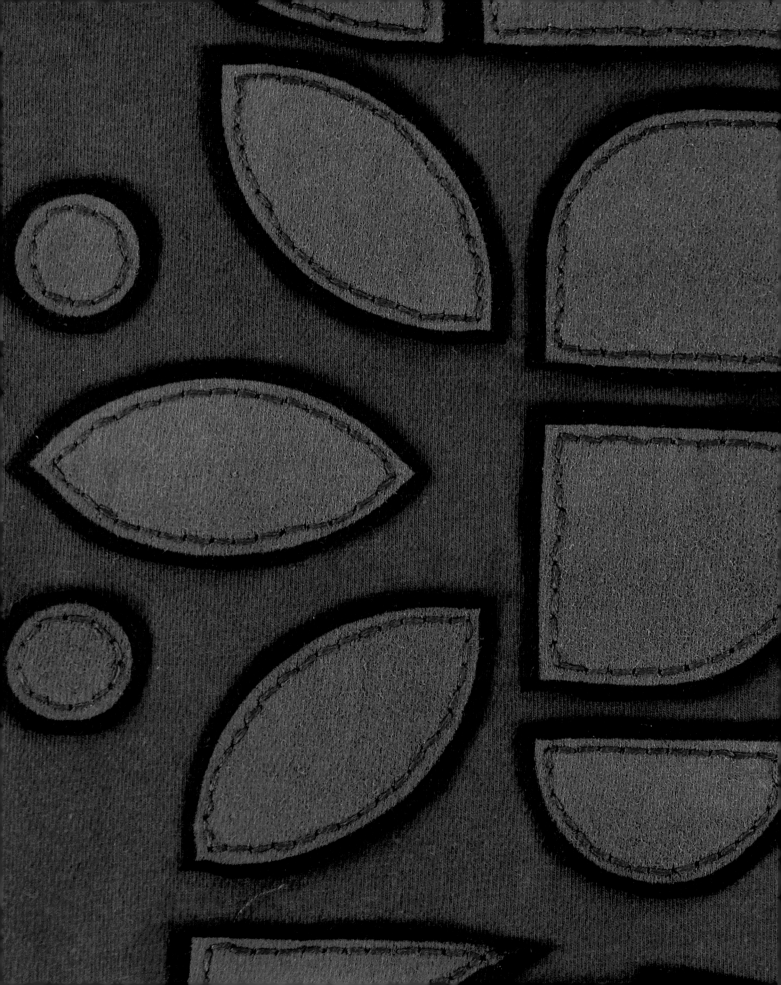

A SIMPLIFIED
GLOSSARY OF COLOR

WHILE I'M FASCINATED BY the complex science of color, I also find that a basic knowledge of color vocabulary helps our teams communicate well and work in union toward a common goal.

Color. A general term used to describe all the hues, tints, and tones.

Color Scale. A scale of a color value with equal steps from dark to light. Sometimes called the value scale.

Color Harmony. A subjective term that describes an individual's perception that a pair or palette of colors has visual harmony or is pleasing to the eye.

Complementary. Also called contrasting or opposite colors. Describes two colors that appear on opposite sides of the color wheel.

Contrast (Low). Used to describe a small, subtle, or low difference of shades, tints, and tones between two colors. (For example, there is a very low contrast between white fabric and pastel green fabric.)

Contrast (High). Used to describe a large, bold, or high difference of shades, tints, and tones between two colors. (For example, there is a high contrast between white fabric and navy textile paint.)

Gray Scale. A scale of gray with equal steps from black to white. Sometimes called the value scale.

Hue. The dominant color family.

Monochromatic. Shades, tints, and tones of a single color.

Palette. A range or collection of colors.

Scale (or Value). A scale of color with equal steps from dark to light.

Shade. A hue where black is added.

Tint. A hue where white is added.

Tone. A hue where gray is added.

Tonal. Shades, tints, and tones of colors in the same general color group.

OPPOSITE Fabric swatch stenciled with the Abstract pattern (see chapter 6, page 176) before embroidery. All garments and projects from Alabama Chanin and The School of Making use stenciling to apply patterns before embroideries are added to cut fabric pieces.

ABOVE Cut garment pattern pieces for the A-Line Dress using the Abstract pattern in Navy, The School of Making; garments are first cut from organic cotton jersey, stenciled, embroidered using a variety of techniques (see page 230 for more on techniques), and then constructed as the final step.

OPPOSITE Fabric swatch detail, Abstract in Navy, backstitch negative reverse appliqué, The School of Making

CHAPTER 6
REPEAT

CAVE ART DATING BACK more than 37,000 years includes evidence of finely crushed pigment blown around the shape of a hand to create a stenciled outline. These stenciled handprints, patterned in repeat, have been found around the globe and are sometimes accompanied by natural motifs taken from daily life: Animals, hunting scenes, and ritual all figure prominently.

A simple way to reproduce the same pattern over and over again, stenciled patterns and motifs appear historically in places like Egyptian tombs and the walls of Pompeii. As the use of the method evolved, makers developed elaborate patterns with multiple layers and colors used for everyday objects like books, playing cards, wallpaper, furniture, and, of course, fabric. By the early twentieth century, and as craftspeople moved to mass-production methods, stencil motifs nevertheless continued to influence design across both public and private sectors. Stenciled and stencil-inspired works show up in public buildings, homes, streetscapes, trains, graffiti, museums, and contemporary art.

Designing a stencil can be as simple as tracing a handprint or a circle (The School of Making's beloved Polka Dot) or preparing a complex, multilayered, interlocking pattern; however, it starts with a simple formula:

> A dot makes up the points of a line.
> A line creates the edge of a shape.
> Shapes make up the parts of a motif.
> Motifs make up the parts of a pattern.
> A grid structures the pattern in never-ending repetition.

OPPOSITE Graphic design for the Abstract stencil. See the final stencil artwork on page 188, and learn more about designing stencils on page 250.

FOLLOWING Fabric swatch, Palm in Gilded Black, stenciled by hand-painting, Alabama Chanin

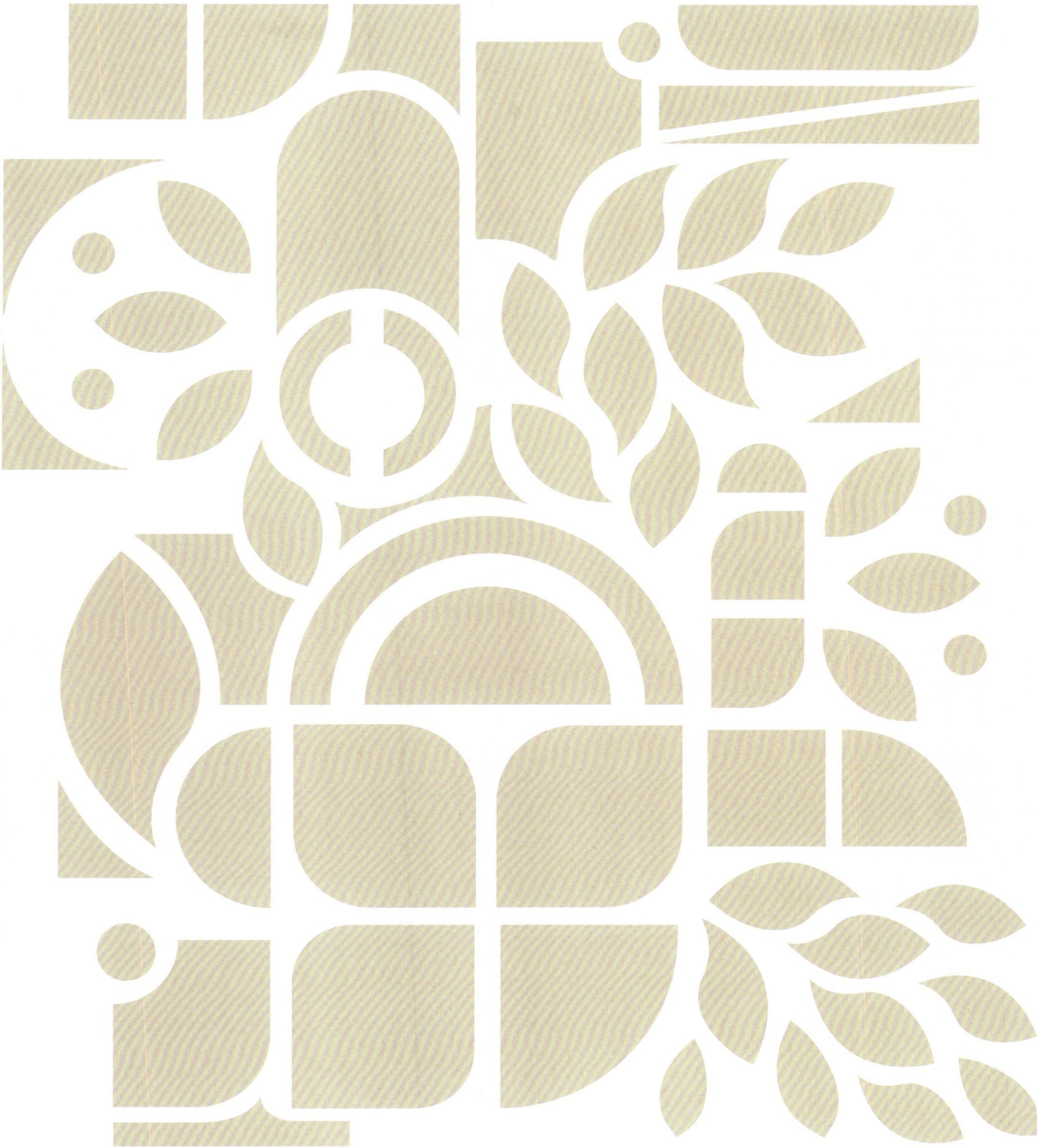

STEN·CIL

sten-suhl

NOUN

1.

A device for applying a pattern, design, words, etc.,
to a surface, consisting of a thin sheet of cardboard, metal, or
other material from which figures or letters have been cut out
and a coloring substance, ink, etc., rubbed, brushed, or pressed over
the sheet, passing through the perforations and onto the surface.

2.

The letters, designs, etc., produced on a surface by this method.

VERB (USED WITH OBJECT)

1.

To mark or paint (a surface) by means of a stencil.

2.

To produce (letters, figures, designs, etc.) by means of a stencil.

MOTIF AND PATTERN

AS THE COLLECTIONS EVOLVED, single motifs applied to T-shirts became repeated patterns that served as the road map our artisans used for applying embroideries and appliqué techniques to our cotton jersey garments. The basis for lean-method manufacturing, stencils allowed us to make only what was ordered or needed—known today as just-in-time manufacturing. The airbrushed patterns became part of the signature style of our fabrics, embroideries, garments, and collections. The company grew quickly and, as was the trend at that time, looked to double sales every year—if not more often. Our small T-shirt operation grew, then collapsed, and was reimagined into Alabama Chanin as it exists today.

In 2007, we moved from the 1,800-square-foot house at Lovelace Crossroads to The Factory. Our new studio was a 5,000-square-foot industrial room that was part of a 120,000-square-foot building—one of the many buildings of this size that had been a hub of textile activity just a decade before—at the center of the T-shirt capital of the world.

The additional space to spread out our production operations was an exciting development that allowed us to design larger and larger stencil patterns on tables made for stenciling fabric yardages and expanded cut-garment pieces. We also organized and built a variety of storage units to contain—and better care for—our growing stencil library. Also, our design studio was set up right beside production, meaning the process from ideas to finished products was streamlined and integrated. In this space, our patterns and how we interpreted them became more complex and layered. The use of one stencil became two, and two became three. And while we once only used an airbrush for stenciling our designs, we slowly began to use brushes, spray bottles, sponges, and an array of other tools for hand-painting garments and fabrics.

With this new capability for more elaborate stencil designs, I reached back into my design school education and used lessons, learned long ago, to explore pattern design and repetition across larger surfaces. The patterns developed during this time remain some of our most beloved. Sometimes I would gaze over my studio table at the words of Georgia O'Keeffe, which I'd posted on the wall: "I found I could say things with color and shapes that I couldn't say any other way." This sentiment became inherent to all we do.

OPPOSITE Fabric swatch, Abstract in Black, backstitch negative reverse appliqué, The School of Making

ANATOMY
OF A STENCIL

THERE ARE MANY BOOKS ON historical and contemporary stencil design that provide patterns intended for private, individual use. Both practical and inspiring, study of these books informed me as I began working with stencils. *Alabama Stitch Book* (see page 260) includes projects created with the Rooster Stencil, originally found in the clip-art book *Ready-to-Use Animal Silhouettes*, by Ellen Sandbeck, and reprinted with permission from Dover Books. Alongside the Rooster, *Alabama Stitch Book* also includes a single motif of the Bloomers pattern as a tear-out, laser-cut, paper stencil. This pattern, from our archives, was originally inspired by a French lace pattern on a pair of antique bloomers purchased from a flea market decades ago, and is still an integral part of The School of Making. Use of preexisting stencils can be a calculated design decision or a jumping-off point in the design process.

The Abstract stencil, one of the most beloved patterns in The School of Making, was an inspired marriage of Bloomers, Polka Dot, and Tony, a pattern of organic shapes originally designed for the Alabama Chanin collection. Find these stencils on the following pages.

RIGHT Fabric swatch, Polka Dots in Parchment, negative reverse appliqué, embroidered using the Feather Stitch from *The Geometry of Hand-Sewing*, The School of Making

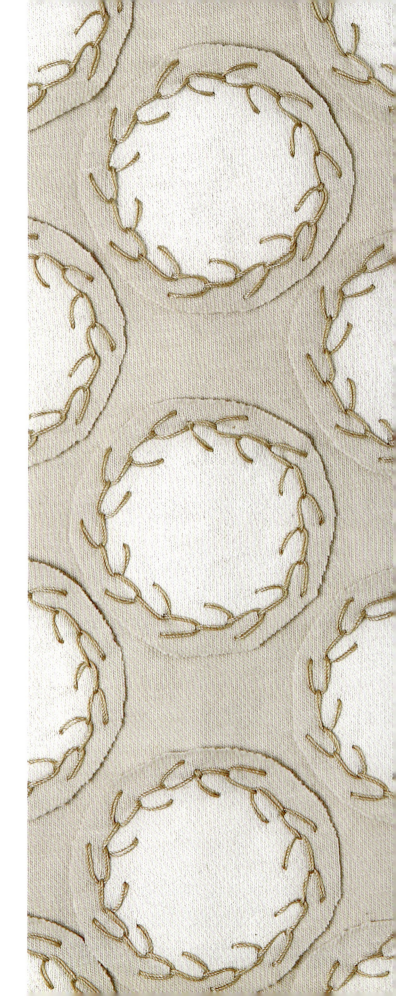

Polka Dot Stencil Artwork

To create the fabrics and garments in this book, The Medium Polka Dot stencil was enlarged by 526 percent. This artwork can be photocopied and enlarged from this page, or visit http://alabamachanin.com for physical stencils and downloadable artwork that can be printed to scale. Artwork size: 22 × 37 inches; stencil size with border: 31 × 46 inches.

Find fabrics in this book using the Polka Dot stencil on pages 1 and 182–183.

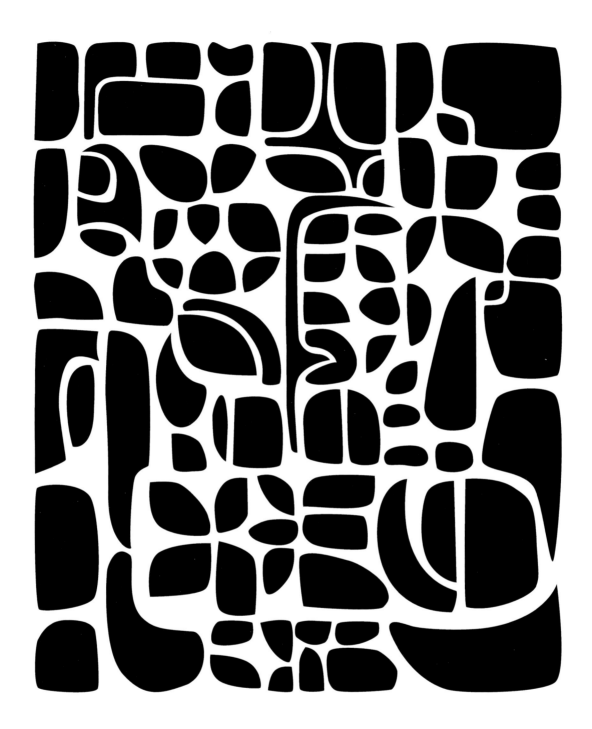

Tony Stencil Artwork

To create the fabrics and garments in this book, The Tony stencil was enlarged by 400 percent. This artwork can be photocopied and enlarged from this page, or visit http://alabamachanin.com for physical stencils and downloadable artwork that can be printed to scale. Artwork size: 22 × 28 inches; stencil size with border: 28 × 34 inches.

Find fabrics in this book using the Tony stencil on pages 76-77, 99, 100-101, and 186-187.

FOLLOWING Fabric swatch, Tony in Black and Ochre, double negative reverse appliqué, Alabama Chanin

Abstract Stencil Artwork

To create the fabrics and garments in this book, the Abstract stencil was enlarged by 455 percent. This artwork can be photocopied and enlarged from this page, or visit http://alabamachanin.com for physical stencils and downloadable artwork that can be printed to scale. Artwork size: 31.1 × 27.4 inches; stencil size with border: 35.5 × 31 inches.

Find fabrics in this book using the Abstract stencil on pages 6, 10, 31, 161-171, 174-175, 180, 192, 193, 246, 248-249

Bloomers Stencil Artwork

To create the fabrics and garments in this book, Bloomers was enlarged by 278 percent. This artwork can be photocopied and enlarged from this page, or visit http://alabamachanin.com for physical stencils and downloadable artwork that can be printed to scale. Artwork size: 18 × 31 inches; stencil size with border: 24 × 35 inches.

Find fabrics in this book using the Bloomers stencil on pages 55, 56, 57 and 92-93.

ABOVE TOP TO BOTTOM The Abstract stencil design was put into a repeat pattern for creating fabric yardage using a rectangular grid. In the one-row repeat as shown above, two stencil motifs are placed horizontally to fit across the 60-inch width of cotton jersey yardage. Below, two adjoined stencils have been aligned to create a never-ending repeating pattern.

OPPOSITE A repeating pattern of four stencils rotated 180 degrees to create a variation of the original—used for Stella's Room on the following pages (read Stencil Transfer on page 256 in the Techniques and Instructions section for more about using stencils)

ABOVE AND OPPOSITE The repeating Abstract stencil on the previous page was chosen by Natalie's granddaughter Stella to pattern her room. Painted with a 3-inch brush using a vertical grid repeat

A SHORT(ISH) GLOSSARY OF VISUAL LITERACY

UNDERSTANDING THE LANGUAGE of visual design is a fundamental of design education. Developing visual literacy is the undertaking of both an education and, I would argue, a lifetime. As a student, I once spent a semester exploring, defining, and attempting to find consensus on a collection of simple terms used in basic design. With a group of other design students, we discussed, probed, and, at times, argued definitions as design principles. It was revelatory—and significant—how differently these seemingly straightforward words were interpreted between individuals and across disciplines. Something as simple as *repeat* was understood as two or more by some, and three or more by others. Heated conversations aside, there was rarely a complete consensus. Discussions of *harmony* lasted a week, and the word was eventually deemed too subjective to be used with authority. Recently I was reminded by one of my fellow students that while *harmony* may be subjective, *unity* is a well-known design principle under Gestalt theory. "See," he wrote, "we are still arguing."

The lexicon of visual design encompasses a large and complicated body of ideas that, like color, can be subjective. Still, never one to shy from a challenge, I continue to explore these concepts, constantly in pursuit of understanding design language. There is no formula—no secret sauce. However, I do believe that understanding the basics of visual language and having well-defined, objective definitions provides structure when designing a pattern or stencil. A relatively consistent design vocabulary also allows for the transfer of knowledge and, when combined with the subjectivity of choosing a color palette, provides patterns, concepts, and ideas for multiple lifetimes of creative pursuit.

The ideas

Dot. A round mark that can be used alone or in a series to create a line.

Form. Describes when a flat, two-dimensional plane becomes three-dimensional either visually, through illusion, or physically.

Geometric Shape. While all shapes are geometric, we use this word to describe primitive geometric shapes that are recognizable and can be defined by geometric terminology such as circle, square, triangle, octagon, etc. These identifiable shapes are commonly understood within culture and can be reasonably predicted. See Organic Shape and Random Shape, below.

Grid. A pattern of regularly or irregularly spaced lines that forms a structure that can be used as a map to order and/or repeat a design.

Grid Structure. A structure for organizing a design, motif, or element in repetition. There are three basic grid structures: square, half-drop, and random. These three structures can be combined and modified through scale, proportion, and spacing to create endless variety.

Interval. Describes the distance between elements or motifs in repetition. As in music, the interval of visual elements can be in succession close together, far apart, or varying in sequence.

Line. A narrow mark or band that can be curved or straight and is the basis for all shapes, motifs, drawings, and grid structures.

Motif. An individual design or graphic pattern that can be repeated in a grid structure to create a patterned surface.

Movement. An implied visual path a viewer's eye takes through a design, pattern, or motif.

Negative Space. The background that surrounds the perceived subject or main graphic element in a design, motif, or pattern.

Organic Shape. A shape, often inspired by nature, that appears random and cannot be reasonably predicted. Some argue that all shapes are organic—including primary geometric shapes. See Geometric Shape, opposite, and Random Shape, below.

Point. Defines a position in space.

Positive Space. The perceived subject or main graphic element in a design, motif, or pattern.

Positive/Negative Space. A relationship between the main graphic element or area in a design or motif and the background that surrounds the perceived subject.

Proportion. The understanding of individual parts of a design, motif, or pattern in relative size, dimension, and relation to one another.

Proximity. Elements or motifs that are placed together so they are perceived as a group because of being located close to one another.

Random Shape. A shape or series of shapes that are not instantly recognizable and cannot be reasonably predicted. Some may ask here, "Can there be a random geometric pattern?" I would answer, "Yes, I have borne witness to both geometric random shapes and random geometrics."

Repeat or Repetition. To replicate a shape or motif two or more times. Some believe that a repetition begins at three of the same shape or motif.

Scale. The overall size of a shape, motif, or design element.

Similarity. Elements or motifs with the same attribute (color, geometry, orientation, etc.) that are perceived as a group because of their sameness.

Space (or Spacing). The area between two shapes, motifs, or design elements. Also see Interval, above.

Stencil. A thin template with a pattern or letters cut out that can be used to transfer a pattern to a surface by applying ink or paint through the cut holes.

Stencil Design (Placement). A stencil that is used to place a single motif or design in a specific area.

Stencil Design (Allover). A stencil that is created with a motif in repeat and is used to completely cover a surface with a pattern.

Texture. The visual appearance or physical feel of a surface. Visual texture uses marks, lines, dots, or shapes to create the illusion of a three-dimensional surface. Fabric and other textiles have an inherent texture that is created by the physics of the fiber at a microscopic level, in combination with the manufacturing processes. (See pages 141–143 for more on the physics of fabrics.)

CHAPTER 7

ROAD MAPS

IF THERE IS ONE THING I can teach my children, it's that there is a long road between points A and B. In Euclidian geometry, a line is an interval between two points that can be extended indefinitely in two directions. In the beginning, an idea is like a straight line: A goes to B, this begets that. However, it is my experience that the line is rarely straight. The development and realization of an idea moves from A to Z, then back to C, and includes all the points between. This is the way of work and life. In our best moments, in flow, the movement between these infinite points is where design happens. This is a journey to the unknown, taking a chance, overcoming fear, embracing discovery, and the miraculous adventure that unfolds. My design professor, educational mentor, and friend Michael Pause was known for saying, "You never know when you might discover something new."

OPPOSITE Chain stitches around the outside of a stencil shape create a web texture and secure the outer Camel-colored layer of cotton jersey to the Wax-colored backing layer that is revealed through cutting away the entire stenciled fabric. This technique is called Outside Reverse Appliqué. (Read more about Outside Reverse Appliqué and other techniques on page 228 in the Techniques and Instructions section.) Fabric swatch, Lace in Camel and Wax, Chain Stitch outside reverse appliqué, Alabama Chanin.

FOLLOWING The Flora pattern incorporates multiple techniques such as couching, appliqué, reverse appliqué, outside reverse appliqué, embroidery, and beading. Fabric swatch, Flora in Wax, Butter Yellow, Pink, Camel, and Natural, assorted techniques, Alabama Chanin

PREVIOUS Fabric swatch, Job Flowers and Cogs, Moss Green, crochet shapes of wool yarn, appliqué, reverse appliqué, and beading

OPPOSITE AND ABOVE Eva's skirt in Job Flowers and Cogs, Alabama Chanin; stencil design for Eyelet Flowers by Eva Whitechapel for Alabama Chanin

SUSTAIN

WITH AN UNDERSTANDING of our craft, processes, artisans, materials, tools, and production systems, we began developing collections at a speed that fit the fashion system. Twice a year we presented collections that were loosely considered fall/winter or spring/summer—which seems simplistic by today's impossible standards of six, or more, collections in a twelve-month span. Our products were being sold around the world, so included work that might be suitable for an Australian summer (in North American winter), and that might be suitable for colder climates while intense heat permeated the Alabama summertime. The world was getting smaller by the day, fueled by the rapid speed at which the internet continued to unfold. Humanity began to connect across all geographies, genders, races, and economies. The possibility of mass consumption grew at lighting speed.

As an organization, we stretched all possible resources to keep up . . . and eventually broke. There is this idea that something always comes from nothing, and that sentiment holds true here because from the broken remains, a new organization was formed that chose to focus on slow growth, community, organic materials, and living wages.

LEFT Use of fabric scraps, upcycled for embroidery, creates texture through a warp and weft placement in the Alabama Tweed fabric swatch, Gilded White Gold, appliqué, embroidery, and beading, Alabama Chanin

OPPOSITE AND ABOVE The Victoria fabric in Navy is a combination of hand-painting, appliqué, embroidery, and beading. Made from organic cotton jersey and terry, with cotton jersey pulls (see page 237) used as couching along with a couched chenille yarn, Alabama Chanin; Lois Coat in the Navy Victoria pattern along with Cadence Rib Dress in Navy, hand-painted, appliqué, embroidery, and beading, organic cotton terry, jersey, and rib fabrics, Alabama Chanin

FOLLOWING Fabric swatch, Pansy in Navy and Concrete, negative reverse appliqué, Alabama Chanin

ABOVE Gina Smock, Lee in tone-on-tone Vetiver with reverse appliqué and beading, Alabama Chanin

OPPOSITE Fabric swatch, Lee in Vetiver, Soft Brown, and Natural, appliqué and embroidery, organic cotton jersey with organic brown grown woven cotton, Alabama Chanin

OPPOSITE Fabric swatch, 21 Years, Navy, hand-painted, Alabama Chanin. The 21 Years stencil was designed as a montage of beloved stencils from across two decades. The stencil archive at Alabama Chanin and The School of Making contains more than 800 stencils that reflect the history of the companies.

ABOVE From the simple early T-shirts created from recycled garments, elaborate hand-embroidered garments evolved and became the core of the work. Today, guests travel from all over the world to Florence, Alabama, to browse the fabric swatch library and be fitted for one-of-a-kind heirloom dresses, jackets, coats, and skirts. Lisa's Dress, Squares in Navy, appliqué, reverse appliqué, embroidery, and beading, organic cotton jersey and upcycled cotton jersey T-shirts, Alabama Chanin

MAKESHIFT, THREADWAYS, AND CONNECTION

I'VE COME TO APPRECIATE the ways in which making and wearing, designer and citizen, come together in communities and spaces. In my design training, we never really spoke directly about the cultural impact of the things (products) we were making. Conversations tended more toward how culture impacted us as designers. I learned to make dresses and thought about the manufacturing process that follows good design, but it took me years to understand that the process of manufacturing has its own inherent culture, its own language, and its own trajectory that is completely separate from me as a designer. At the end of the making process, these products go out into the world and become a part of someone else's life, creating a never-ending cycle of connection between designer, maker, and user.

For this reason, we founded Project Threadways. Inspired by the work of the Center for the Study of Southern Culture and the Southern Foodways Alliance, the purpose of the organization is to record, study, and explore the history of textiles by seeking to understand the impact that this material culture and its creation—from raw material to finished good—had and has on our local community, region, nation, and global community, connecting the people, places, and materials throughout the process.

From 2012 to 2015, Alabama Chanin hosted a series of workshops and conversations called Makeshift, seeking to understand how the act of making brings together the worlds of fashion, craft, design, and DIY to enhance communities. Asking these questions led to a vibrant dialogue with scholars, designers, and makers about material culture. This scholarly conversation transformed into a larger undertaking: Project Threadways.

I could not have imagined in 2000, standing on that New York street corner, the vibrant community of makers and citizens that awaited me at home. In the same way, my grandmothers could not have imagined the rock 'n' roll and global textile production to come. And yet, in all of it is a hidden thread of connection, of craft, and of our common community.

OPPOSITE In 2021, Alabama Chanin collaborated with Diana Weymar of Tiny Pricks Project to create a collection of twenty-one one-of-a-kind jackets. Each piece was embroidered with twenty-one verses written by Diana and Natalie that capture Alabama Chanin's journey and evolution over the past twenty-one years. See a detail of the poem on page 258 and a stencil used to embroider the full poem on page 259. The 21 Years Jacket, Camel, embroidery, Alabama Chanin

"The stories of factories and families were beautiful and devastating in equal measure. And as the work evolved, I understood that we were creating not just collections, but also a model for how to design and grow a fashion business in a sustainable way. In a world of fast fashion, mass production, and machines, I wanted to work slowly and thoughtfully; I wanted to contribute to my community."

—NATALIE CHANIN

(See page 118)

OPPOSITE Fabric swatch, "Chunky Rib," reverse appliqué organic cotton jersey and rib fabrics, Alabama Chanin.

ABOVE "Minis" was developed to use every scrap of fabric in the production process. Tiny squares of cotton jersey cut into half-inches are sewn in stripes to create the effect of a woven tweed fabric. This fabric development was the work of the entire production team, from cutting and stenciling to the talented artisans who sewed each scrap to the garments. It took our whole community to make this work possible. Fabric swatch, "Minis" in Mixed Grey, appliqué, Alabama Chanin

A MAP OF
THE WORLD

THE WORD *ARTISAN*, mostly used as a noun, nevertheless implies action: one who is trained to make. Historically, artisanship included a process from apprentice to journeyman or -woman, to mastery of a craft. In her book *Deluxe: How Luxury Lost Its Luster*, Dana Thomas writes about this process with the fashion house Hermès. The company "requires that all newly hired leather artisans—most of whom have graduated from one of France's renowned leatherworking academies— spend two years as apprentices in its own schools . . . to learn from Hermès's senior leather craftsmen how to cut skins and sew the house's signature saddle stitch perfectly."

Master gardeners often speak of the "fourth dimension," that being time. There is an old garden saying I learned as a child: "The first year it sleeps, the second year it creeps, and the third year it leaps." It needs time to settle, time for the momentum of building roots, and, finally, time to grow and keep growing.

Learning to do something well takes time. To become a master takes even more time. This idea of time and training as critical to the process of making a product well has been lost in today's fast economy (fast food, fast fashion, fast housing). Quality and community being the sacrifices we make when we choose the fast version.

Twenty-one years in, we have slowly developed a fabric-swatch library that has more than one thousand swatches of patterns, techniques, color variations, and inspiration. While there are no road maps for how to approach design, there is a map, of sorts, for discovering this world. On pages 222–223, there is a map for one fabric that is where all of our work begins. On pages 266–269, there is information about our design choices, pictures, process, and people who have inspired this work.

Take your time. Settle in. The journey is most certainly the destination.

OPPOSITE The Rosanne Coat, Beaded Sylvan in Dove, Alabama Chanin.

FOLLOWING SPREADS Fabric swatch, Beaded Sylvan in Concrete, appliqué, reverse appliqué, embroidery, and beading, Alabama Chanin; fabric map for Beaded Sylvan showing where to add stitches, appliqué, beading, and reverse appliqué; fabric swatch, Sylvan in Black (without beads), appliqué, reverse appliqué, and French knots, Alabama Chanin

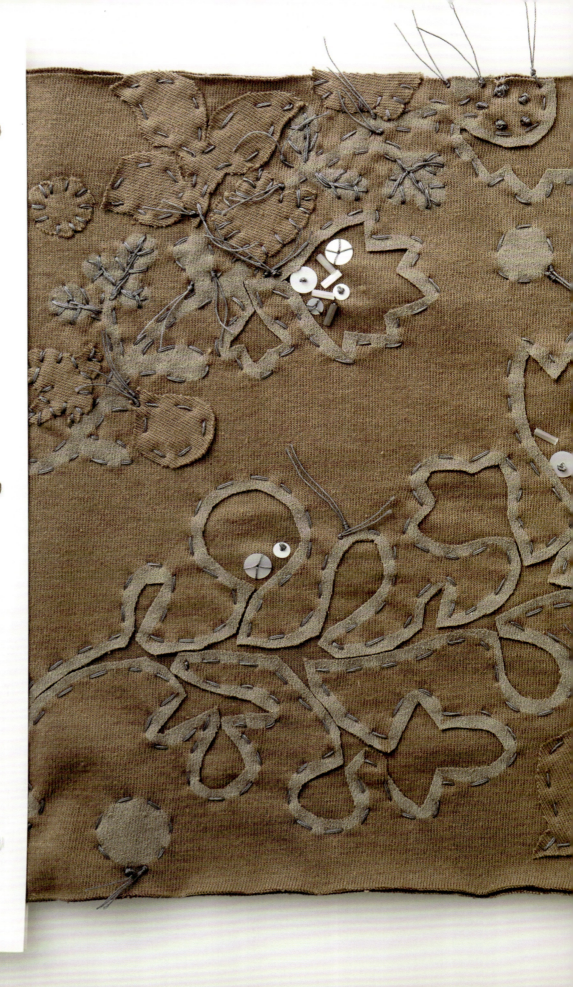

#26386 Beaded Sylvan

ALABAMA
CHANIN

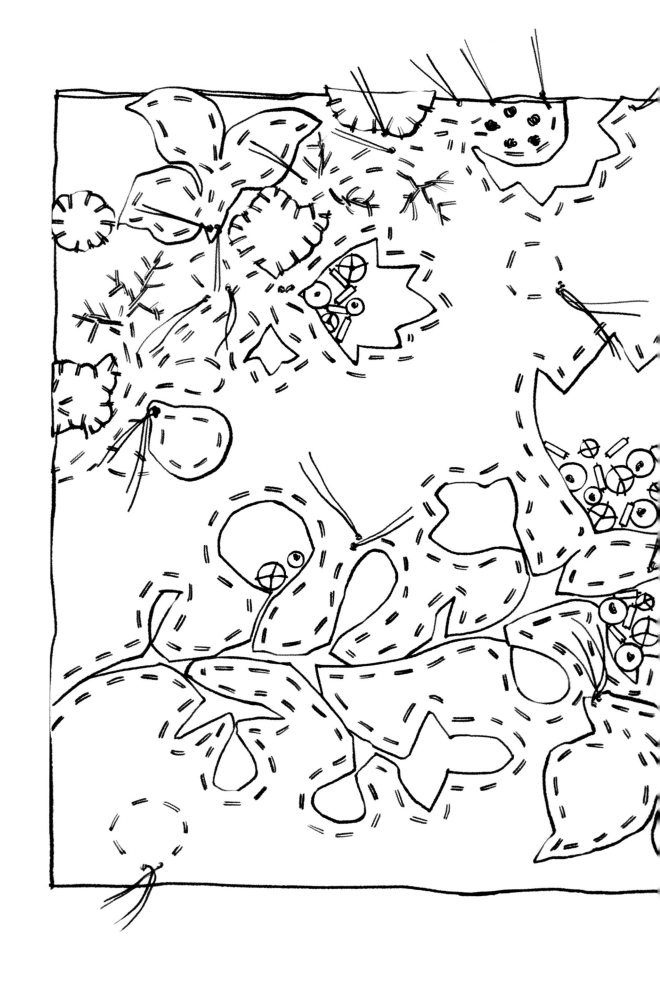

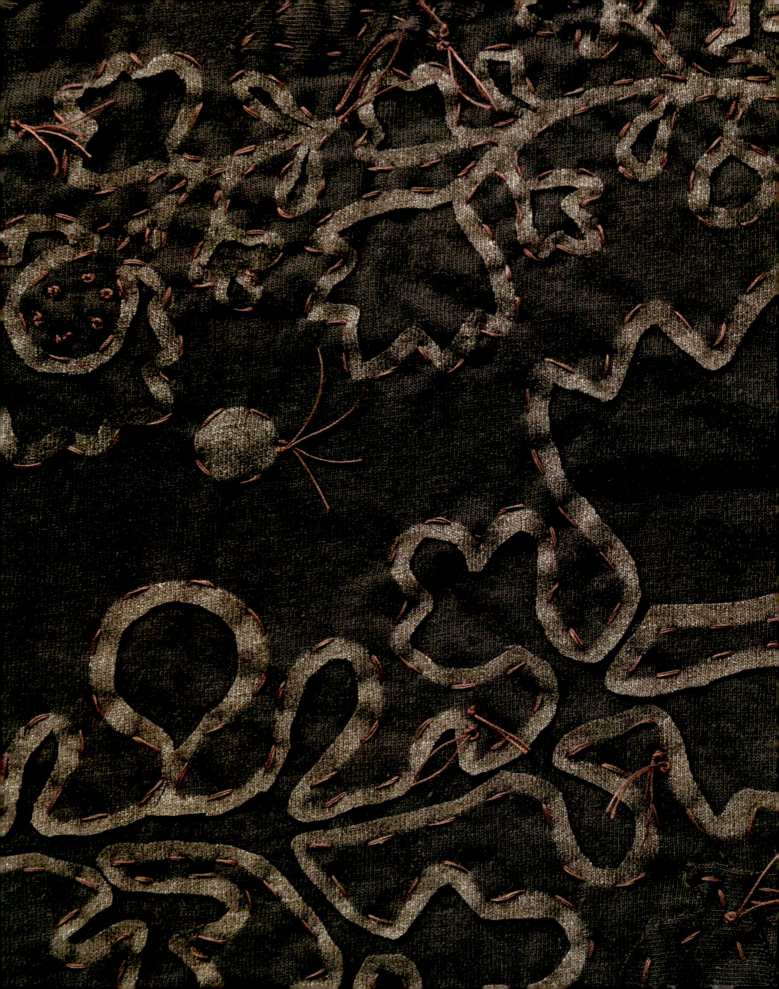

SOURCES AND FURTHER READING

P. 12: Rosanne Cash, "A Feather Finds a Bird"

Copyright ©2014, originally published on Alabama Chanin: 21 Years website, reprinted by permission of Writers House LLC acting as agent for the author. https://alabamachanin.com/21-years-celebration

P. 14: "A Feather's Not a Bird," from the album *The River & the Thread*

Copyright ©2014 by Rosanne Cash and John Leventhal, published by Chelcait Music (SESAC) administered by Hipgnosis Songs Group and Lev-A-Tunes (ASCAP) administered by Downtown Music Publishing. Reprinted by permission of Writers House LLC acting as agent for the author

PP. 16-17: Rosanne Cash x The School of Making collaboration inspired by "A Feather's Not a Bird" and *Bird on a Blade* by Rosanne Cash and Dan Rizzie

Rosanne Cash, Dan Rizzie, *Bird on a Blade*, University of Texas Press, 2018

PP. 19-23: Learn more about The Moth: themoth.org

Read books from The Moth:

Catherine Burns and Neil Gaiman, *All These Wonders: True Stories About Facing the Unknown*, book 1 of 2: The Moth Presents, Crown, 2017

Catherine Burns and Meg Wolitzer, *Occasional Magic: True Stories About Defying the Impossible*, book 2 of 2: The Moth Presents, 2019

Meg Bowles, Catherine Burns, Jenifer Hixson, et al., *How to Tell a Story: The Essential Guide to Memorable Storytelling from The Moth,* Crown, 2022

P. 19: *Lost & Found Sound*, "Route 66: The Mother Road," The Kitchen Sisters, National Public Radio, 1984. Learn more about *Lost & Found Sound*: www.kitchensisters. org/stories/lost-found-sound/

P. 19: Read more from the Kitchen Sisters:

Nikki Silva, Davia Nelson, foreword by Alice L. Waters, *Hidden Kitchens: Stories, Recipes, and More*, Rodale Books, 2005

P. 20: Listen to Michael J. "Mike" Massimino's story "A View of the Earth," told at The Moth, November 14, 2012: themoth.org/storytellers/michael-j-massimino

Read his story: Mike Massimino, *Spaceman: An Astronaut's Unlikely Journey to Unlock the Secrets of the Universe*, Crown, 2016

P. 20: Pema Chödrön, *When Things Fall Apart: Heart Advice for Difficult Times*, Shambhala, 1996

P. 33: Laird Borrelli-Persson, "From Marlon Brando to Kendall Jenner, 27 of the Best Classic White T-Shirts Ever," *Vogue*, May 20, 2015, https://www.vogue.com/ article/best-classic-white-t-shirts-of-all-time

P. 33: Paola Antonelli and Michelle Fisher, eds., *Items: Is Fashion Modern?*, The Museum of Modern Art, 2017

P. 49: Richard Sennett, *The Craftsman*, Yale University Press, 2009

PP. 52-55: Excerpt from an interview with Michi Meko for the 21 Years project. Read the full interview: https:// alabamachanin.com/21-years-celebration/michi-meko-collaboration-2004. Learn more about his work: http:// michimeko.com/

P. 58: Learn more about Rick Hall, FAME Studios, the Muscle Shoals Rhythm Section, Muscle Shoals Sound Studios, and the community's rich musical heritage in the documentary film *Muscle Shoals* by Greg "Freddy" Camalier and Stephen M. Badger, Magnolia Pictures, 2013

P. 58: Charlotte Brunel, with a foreword by Bruno Collin, *The T-Shirt Book*, Assouline Publishing, 2002

P. 58: Stephanie Kramer, contributor, in Paola Antonelli and Michelle Millar Fisher, eds., *Items: Is Fashion Modern?*, The Museum of Modern Art, 2017

P. 58: Read about the Rolling Stones' "Hot Lips" T-shirt: www.nytimes.com/2020/04/13/arts/design/rolling-stones-logo-anniversary.html

P. 70: Ruth Stone's story of capturing poems is beautifully told in this book:

Elizabeth Gilbert, *Big Magic: Creative Living Beyond Fear*, Riverhead Books, 2015

P. 70: Rollo May, "Commitment is healthiest when it is not without doubt but in spite of doubt," in *The Courage to Create*, W. W. Norton & Co., 1975

PP. 72-80: "Hidden Spaces," Muscle Shoals National Heritage Area, University of North Alabama Public History Center and History Department, River Heritage Area, photography by Abraham Rowe. Muscle Shoals National Heritage Area preserves and promotes cultural heritage across six counties of the Tennessee River basin. Learn more: https://hiddenspaces.org/

P. 82: Alabama Chanin, *Stitch: The Film*, 2000. Watch the film: alabamachanin.com/2016/01/stitch-a-22-minute-documentary/

PP. 84-85: Sissi Farassat, *Sioseh 17: Alabama*, self-published, 2001

P. 105: Photo of framed antique Fishing and Boating Map of Tennessee River, Edstan Map Company, ca. 1950, courtesy of Billy Smith

P. 105: Wilson Dam, Historic American Engineering Record, Creator, and Tennessee Valley Authority. Wilson Dam & Hydroelectric Plant, Spanning Tennessee River at Wilson Dam Road Route 133, Muscle Shoals, Colbert County, AL. trans by Behrens, Tommitter Documentation Compiled After. Photograph. Retrieved from the Library of Congress, www.loc.gov/item/al1052/

P. 105: Electric Towers, Studio Job @ Project Alabama Collaboration, graphic for fabrics, 2005

P. 109: Mihály Csikszentmihályi, *Flow: The Psychology of Optimal Experience*, Harper Perennial Modern Classics, 2008

P. 124: Norton Juster, *The Dot and the Line: A Romance in Lower Mathematics*, Random House, 1963

PP. 132-137: Quote from Anni Albers's "Material as Metaphor" lecture for the panel *The Art/Craft Connection: Grass Roots or Glass Houses* at the College Art Association's annual meeting, New York, February 25, 1982

PP. 132-137: Josef and Anni Albers's living room, photograph courtesy of the Western Regional Archives, State Archives of North Carolina, and the Josef and Anni Albers Foundation

PP. 132-137: Anni Albers quote courtesy of the Josef and Anni Albers Foundation: albersfoundation.org/

P. 152: Michael T. Morrall, *History and Description of Needle Making*, Balmoral House, 1862

P. 152: John G. Rollins, *Needlemaking*, Shire, 2008

P. 152: Jo-Ann Gloger and Patrick Chester, *More to a Needle Than Meets the Eye: A Brief History of Needlemaking, Past and Present*, Forge Mill Needle Museum, 1999, forgemill.org.uk/web/

P. 152: Additional reading:

Mary C. Beaudry, *Findings: The Material Culture of Needlework and Sewing*, Yale University, London, 2007

Rozsika Parker, *The Subversive Stitch Embroidery and the Making of the Feminine*, I. B. Tauris & Co., New York, 2010

P. 160: Isaac Newton, *Opticks: Or, A Treatise of the Reflections, Refractions, Inflections, and Colours of Light*, 1666

P. 160: Narayan Khandekar, and Victoria Finlay, *An Atlas of Rare & Familiar Colour: The Harvard Art Museums' Forbes Pigment Collection*, Atelier Éditions, 2019

P. 181: "I found I could say things with color and shapes that I couldn't say any other way." Georgia O'Keeffe. Georgia O'Keeffe Museum: okeeffemuseum.org/visual-vocabulary/

P. 182: Ellen Sandbeck, *Ready-to-Use Animal Silhouettes*, Dover Books, 1989

P. 184: Patrick Syme, *Werner's Nomenclature of Colours: Adapted to Zoology, Botany, Chemistry, Mineralogy, Anatomy, and the Arts*, 1821

P. 184: "In order to use color effectively it is necessary to recognize that color deceives continually."

Josef Albers, *Interaction of Color*, Yale University Press, 1963. This quote courtesy of the Josef and Anni Albers Foundation: albersfoundation.org/

P. 196: "You never know when you might discover something new."

Michael Pause from First Year Studio class at North Carolina State University, College of Design, 1984

Michael Pause, Roger H. Clark, *Precedents in Architecture: Analytic Diagrams, Formative Ideas, and Partis*, Wiley, 1985

P. 219: Dana Thomas, *Deluxe: How Luxury Lost its Luster*, Penguin, 2007

Additional reading: Dana Thomas, *Fashionopolis: The Price of Fast Fashion and the Future of Clothes*, Penguin, 2019

P. 270: Anne Lamott, *Bird by Bird: Some Instructions on Writing and Life*, Pantheon Books, 1994

Additional reading and resources: Alabama Chanin Journal: https://journal.alabamachanin.com/

TECHNIQUES AND INSTRUCTIONS

FROM THE VERY FIRST "Stitch Book" (see page 121) to the expanding Alabama Chanin production, The School of Making workshops, and the Studio Books series (see page 260), documenting the process of making and creating instructions has been both a necessary tool and part of what we call Cultural Sustainability—keeping craft traditions alive in our community and beyond.

The following pages document a small collection of the techniques we utilize for Alabama Chanin collections, how to make our Needle Roll and Sewing Kit, some ideas on Exploration of Color with our organic cotton jersey fabrics, and tips on Stencil Design 101.

RIGHT Transitional embroidery uses a variety of techniques (see the following page) across the face of a fabric swatch, garment, or project. The fabric swatch at right begins with negative reverse appliqué on the left, transitioning to reverse appliqué in the middle, and outside reverse appliqué to the right.

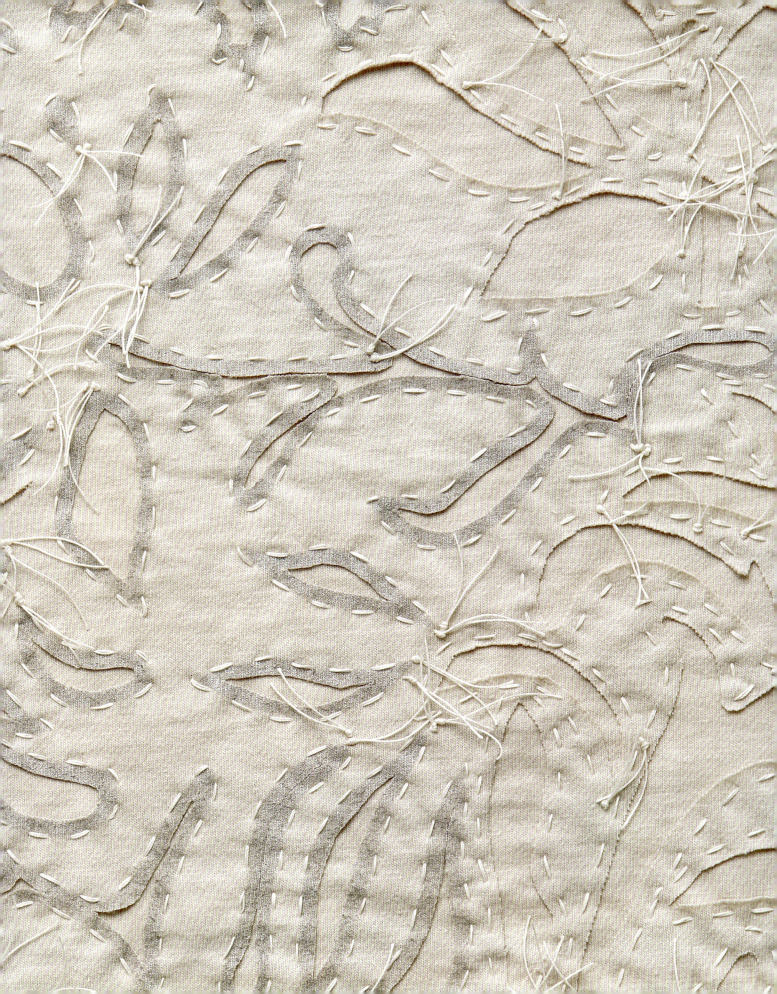

TECHNIQUES

WHILE REVERSE APPLIQUÉ became the cornerstone of our early collections (see page 89), variations of this technique evolved over time. Descriptions of our most frequently used techniques are presented here in alphabetical order. Since we work primarily with organic cotton jersey fabric, these instructions follow the style of our work with The School of Making and Alabama Chanin. Instructions for Reverse Appliqué are found in chapter 2, on page 91. All of the techniques detailed here can be used in a multitude of variations and combinations to accomplish advanced textile and surface designs.

APPLIQUÉ

Appliqué simply means to apply a layer of fabric on top of another layer of fabric. This technique can be two or three layers when complete, depending on the project design. Appliqué can be joined to the base fabric with a wide variety of stitches. As in Quilting and Reverse Appliqué, apply a stencil pattern to a top layer of fabric and add a backing layer. Then, apply a mirror image (wrong side) of the stencil pattern to the back of the appliqué layer. Cut out individual stencil shapes to match the stenciled top layer and pin, stencil-to-stencil. Sew through all three layers with the stitch of choice.

Note that no stencil paint or drawing will be visible when this technique is employed.

See pages 38–39, 126–127, 138–139, and 211 for examples of Appliqué.

COUCHING

In its traditional form, Couching is achieved by laying strands of yarn or another material across the top layer of fabric and then securing into place with a Satin Stitch to create a rounded, sculptural shape. Our form of Couching secures Cotton Jersey Ropes around a stencil shape using a Whipstitch. When adding Couching to a project, make sure to begin and end each shape by securing the rope by stitching through the center at the beginning and end of each shape, then use fingers to hold or sculpt the rope into place while working around the stenciled shape.

See pages 76–77, 198–199, and 206 for examples of Couching.

INKED + QUILTED

Like Quilting, apply a stencil pattern to a top layer of fabric and add a backing layer. Using a permanent or textile marker, trace around the stenciled shape to create a line of desired thickness. Afterward, and similar to Negative Reverse Appliqué, join the two layers with a Straight Stitch ⅛" (3 mm) inside the edge of each stenciled and traced shape.

NEGATIVE REVERSE APPLIQUÉ

Negative Reverse Appliqué looks like Appliqué but is worked like Reverse Appliqué. However, after stenciling and adding a backing layer, use a Straight Stitch ⅛" (3 mm) inside the stenciled shape and then cut away the top layer of fabric ⅛" (3 mm) outside the stenciled shape. This leaves a ¼" (6 mm) sliver of fabric outside of the stitching line.

See pages 31, 162, 170–171, 182–183, and 208–209 for examples of Negative Reverse Appliqué.

OUTSIDE REVERSE APPLIQUÉ

Outside Reverse Appliqué is worked like Reverse Appliqué. However, after stenciling and adding a backing layer, use a Straight Stitch ⅛" (3 mm) outside of the stenciled shape and then cut away the top layer of fabric ⅛" (3 mm) inside the stitching line to remove all of the stenciled pattern.

See pages 197, 198-199, and 228-229 for examples of Outside Reverse Appliqué.

RELIEF APPLIQUÉ

Relief Appliqué is accomplished in the same way as our regular Appliqué but using an appliqué shape that is cut approximately 15 to 20 percent larger than the stencil shape on the top layer of fabric. Forcing the larger appliqué piece into a smaller area creates wrinkles that remain intact after ironing the completed appliqué.

REVERSE APPLIQUÉ

Reverse Appliqué is worked using two layers of fabric. As in Quilting, apply a stencil pattern to a top layer of fabric, add a backing layer, and then join the two layers with a ⅛" (3 mm) to ¼" (6 mm) Straight Stitch around the edge of each stenciled shape. Once the shapes have been stitched, the top layer of fabric inside the stencil shapes is trimmed away to reveal the backing fabric layer. See page 91 for instructions.

See pages 92-93, 144-145, and 161 for examples of Reverse Appliqué.

THREE-DIMENSIONAL EMBROIDERY

This describes a combination of Reverse Appliqué and Appliqué across the face of a project. Additional embroidery stitches, materials, and beads are sometimes added to this technique.

See pages 136, 198-201, 204-205, and 220-225 for examples of Three-Dimensional Embroideries.

TRANSITIONAL EMBROIDERY

Transitional embroidery is created by changing embroidery techniques across the face of a project. Additional embroidery stitches, materials, and beads are sometimes added to this technique.

See page 228 for an example of Transitional Embroidery.

QUILTING

Apply a stencil pattern to a top layer of fabric, add a backing layer, and then join the two layers with an ⅛" (3 mm) to ¼" (6 mm)-long Straight Stitch around the edge of each stenciled shape.

See page 28 for an example of Quilting.

NEEDLE ROLL

THIS SMALL ROLL and cotton jersey pull are made from a double layer of cotton jersey scraps, left over from the sewing process. Instructions below describe how to cut out this project and all projects using cotton jersey.

1 **Make Project Pattern**
Create a paper pattern that is 3 × 9" (7.5 × 23 cm). Label pattern piece and mark grainline running parallel with the 3" (7.5-cm) edge.

2 **Cut Top-Layer Pattern Piece**
Lay out your top-layer fabric and place the paper pattern on top of the fabric, making sure the pattern and fabric grainlines run in the same direction (see page 150). Use tailor's chalk to trace around the pattern's edges, remove the paper pattern, and cut out the traced pattern with fabric scissors, cutting just inside the chalked line to remove it entirely. (Note that we prefer holding or weighting the pattern to pinning it on the fabric, which, in the case of cotton jersey, can skew the fabric and make the cutting uneven.)

3 **Cut Backing-Layer Pattern Piece**
To make a double-layer project, lay the back fabric flat. Repeat step 2, using the cut top-layer piece as pattern guide. You will now have two matching pieces.

4 **Assemble Needle Roll**
Place the back (or wrong) side of each cut fabric piece together to assemble the needle roll. This creates a strip of fabric where the face (or right) side of the fabric is visible on the outside and the inside of the Needle Roll. Add pins and needles and roll up to close.
Note that with most cotton jersey projects at Alabama Chanin and The School of Making, both layers of cut project pieces face in the same direction so that the face of the backing-layer project pieces touches the back (or wrong) side of the top-layer project pieces. When cutting or trimming the top-layer fabric for a reverse appliqué garment, the finished project will have all face- (or right-) side fabric visible when the garment is worn.

5 **Add Cotton Jersey Rope**
Following the instructions for Cotton Jersey Ropes on page 237, cut a strip of jersey ½ × 8" (1.3 × 20 cm) and with the grain of the fabric. Take each cut end in your hands and pull to roll, making sure the rope is evenly rolled from end to end. Cut to a finished length of 9" and tie around your Needle Roll.

TRAVEL KIT BAG

The Travel Kit Bag is the size of the zipper bag I used for sewing supplies when traveling and is the design of the Essential Sewing Kit bag used at The School of Making. When complete, it measures approximately 8½ × 6″ (21.5 × 15 cm) and is the perfect size for one piece of a sewing project, one spool of Button Craft Thread (see page 159), the Needle Roll (see page 232—instructions), and a pair of small embroidery scissors (see page 244—scissors). The project instructions can be used to make bags in a range of sizes for all travel necessities by enlarging or reducing the pattern illustration below.

1   Make Project Pattern

Create a paper pattern that is 17½″ (44.5 cm) tall × 9″ (23 cm) wide. Label the pattern piece and mark grainline running parallel with the 17½″ (44.5 cm) edge.

Add marks along the 17½″ (44.5 cm) edge of paper pattern at 2½″ (6.5 cm), 8½″ (21.5 cm), and 11½″ (29 cm) and label A, B, and C. These are your fold lines. Label top left corner D. (See illustration below.)

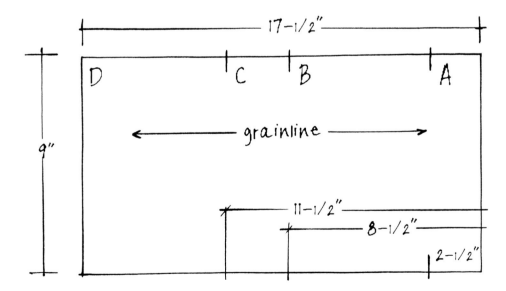

2   **Cut Project Pattern Pieces**

Using your pattern from step 1, cut a top layer and backing layer for your bag in the color of your choice.

Stencil, embellish, embroider, or add any desired decoration.

Lay out project pieces with wrong sides together.

3   **Fold Project Pieces**

Use mark A to fold down 2½" (6.5 cm) as shown in the illustration above. Fold D to meet A and align marks B and C, sandwiching them between the front and back of the project.

4   Using a Straight Stitch (see page 67), sew the sides of the bag together.

5   Turn the bag inside out and fill with a Needle Roll, small scissors, and project in process.

6   Plan your next trip.

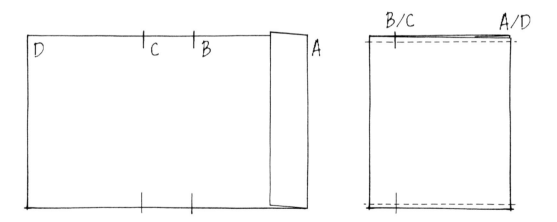

COTTON JERSEY ROPES (OR PULLS)

THE PHYSICS OF HOW cotton jersey is produced, and the way the material reacts to the production process, create a set of circumstances that we often employ when designing projects and garments. Because of the physics of knitting, when jersey fabric is cut across, or against, the grainline, its cut edge will roll to the fabric's right side; conversely, when the fabric is cut with the grainline, its cut edge will roll to the wrong side. Many of our garment designs use this "rolling" process at hems in lieu of hemming. The raw edge creates a rolled hem that happens naturally. This fabric trait can also be used to create "ropes" or "pulls" of cotton jersey by pulling on cut strips of fabric to force the inherent rolling.

Finished ropes can be used in a multitude of ways, including, but not limited to: couching (see page 230), weaving chair seats and backs or fabric, tying up packages, gift wrapping, tie closures for garments, garden ties (see Natalie's garden on page 21)—securing plants to their stakes, lashing sticks together, tying reading glasses around your neck, and a thousand other things.

1 Cut cotton jersey scraps into strips from ½ to 3" (1.3 to 7.5 cm) wide, depending on the desired thickness. Cut across the grain to produce more stretchable ropes where the fabric back is visible. Cut with the grain to create a rope that is slightly less stretchable with the fabric face visible.

2 Holding each end of your cut jersey strips, pull each strip apart to create rolled edges. Work the entire cut strip until it is uniformly rolled from end to end.

ABOVE Needle Roll with Cotton Jersey Rope

TOOL KITS

FOLLOWING ARE LISTS of our design and production tools. Build a tool kit over time as creativity, skill, and projects evolve.

DESIGN TOOLS

Research Library

Journal for organizing ideas

Tracing paper, for designing motifs and repeating patterns

Graph paper, for geometric design

Mechanical pencil

Erasers

6" transparent gridded ruler

Colored pencils and markers

Fabric and paint-color cards and swatches

STITCHING TOOLS

Sewing, Embroidery, and Beading needles in assorted sizes (see Needle Guide on page 156)

Thimbles

Needle-nose pliers, for pulling needles through multiple layers of fabric

Glass-head pins

Tailor's, Dressmaker's, or Spring-loaded Shears for cutting out fabric and projects

5" knife-edge scissors, for smaller cutwork

4" embroidery scissors, for small, detailed cutwork

3½" gold-handled embroidery scissors, for minute cutwork

Seam ripper

PATTERNMAKING AND CUTTING TOOLS

18"–24" plastic gridded ruler

Pattern paper or butcher paper

Styling design ruler, for shaping pattern curves

Tape measure

Measurement worksheets for planning

Cutting mat

Rotary cutter

Craft knife

Paper scissors

STENCILING TOOLS

Medium- or heavyweight transparent film or Mylar, for making stencils

Spray adhesive, for attaching designs to transparent film and for holding stencil in place while transferring design to fabric

Permanent or textile markers, for transferring stencil designs to fabric

Textile paint, for transferring stencil designs to fabric

Paintbrushes (optional), for transferring textile paint to fabric

Clean spray bottles with adjustable nozzles (optional), for transferring textile paint to fabric

Airbrush gun and air compressor (optional), for transferring textile paint to fabric

SCISSOR GUIDE

GARMENT, TAILOR'S, DRESSMAKER'S, OR SPRING-LOADED SHEARS

Shears typically have one straight and one bent-angle blade, a round thumb hole, and an oblong finger hole, and are available in left- and right-handed versions. The bent angle allows you to rest the bottom blade of the scissor on the table while you are working. The bend helps prevent you from lifting the fabric off the table as you cut, reducing fabric slippage, and ensuring a more accurate cut, as well as helping to reduce fatigue when you are doing a lot of cutting. Shears are available in lengths from six to twelve inches (or greater). When looking for the perfect pair of shears for you, it is important to note the feel of the shears in your hand. They should fit your hand's length and have the right amount of tension. You may also find that you prefer one size of shears for a particular type of fabric.

EMBROIDERY SCISSORS

Embroidery scissors have thin, sharp matching blades that range in size from three to four inches and are used for cutting small areas of fabric where great precision is needed. The two sharply pointed tips are perfect for small and/or delicate cutting and trimming threads. There are embroidery scissors with two finger holes—like a normal scissor—and versions with flat, spring-loaded handles like pliers. You may also love the small stork-shaped version that has a curved neck that helps get into hard-to-reach areas for trimming.

KNIFE-EDGE SCISSORS

The knife-edge scissor has one pointed tip on the bottom and one bent tip blade on the top. Also used for cutting small areas of fabric where great precision is required, the knife-edge most commonly comes in four- and five-inch versions.

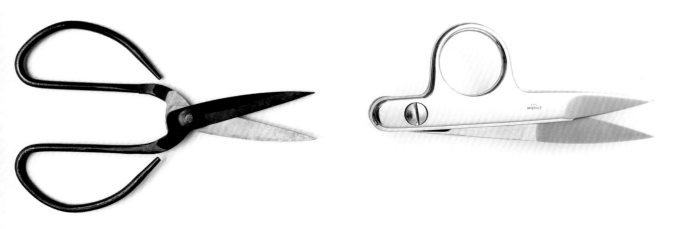

CRAFT SCISSORS

There are many, many scissors available in this genre, from plastic-handled scissors favored by schools to beautiful Japanese-style cutting instruments. The two oval-shaped handles seem perfect for all crafting tasks (they are equally right- or left-handed) and the blades seem to cut vegetables, paper, and, in a pinch, fabric and threads equally well.

SNIPS AND SPECIALITY SCISSORS

There are many different versions of speciality snips and scissors on the market that are perfect for clipping threads and trimming small areas of fabric.

EXPERIMENTING WITH COLOR

EVERY COLLECTION, COLLABORATION, or project begins with choosing a palette of colors to be used in combination with a stencil or fabric design. The process is experimental. Colors and patterns are combined, and recombined, refined, and developed. In the end, a final set of colors is chosen for implementation in the collection. For me, this is the most important, and enjoyable, part of the design process.

For the experimentations in this section, we used the Abstract Stencil (see page 188). See pages 262–269 to review our design choices.

MATERIALS

Cotton jersey fabric in a range of colors

Stencil

Fabric shears

Ruler

Marking tools

Textile paint in a range of colors

Brushes or airbrush supplies for transferring textile paint

Pins

Needles

Button craft thread in a range of colors

Embroidery floss in a range of colors

Embroidery scissors

1   Select a color inspiration or review colors you have available.

2   Select 3 to 4 fabric colors for experimentation.

3   Choose a stencil for experimentation (see chapter 6, beginning on page 176, for more on stencils and stenciling).

4   Cut out 5 to 6 swatches of 4 × 4" (10 × 10 cm) (or larger) from each color.

5   Choose textile paint colors or mix textile paint colors, if desired.

6   Test out the colors on your fabric swatches by painting or airbrushing through your stencil pattern. Let paints dry thoroughly.

Fabric	Thread	Embroidery F
White	White	White
Natural	Cream	Natural
Ballet	Dogwood	Tea
Camel	Dogwood	Tea
Navy	Navy	Navy

onal Paint	Metallic Paint	Heads
Ecru	Pearl Silver	White Armor
Wood	Pearl Silver	Gold Armor
Ecru	Moonlight	White Armor
Wood	Pearl Silver	Gold Armor
Slate	Moonlight	Black Armor

7   Review the test swatches and choose final paint colors.

8   Stencil 2 to 3 swatches of each color in the chosen paint color for the top layer of color-exploration swatches. Let painted swatches dry thoroughly. Follow any manufacturer directions for setting paints to fabric.

9   Choose a backing color and pin the top- and backing-layers together.

10 Choose thread and/or embroidery floss colors.

11 Using the technique of your choice (see page 230 for variations), complete your swatch.

12 Experiment with a variety of color combinations and thread colors.

13 Select color combination and further experiment with a variety of techniques.

14 Review your work and choose your favorite swatch.

15 Cut 10 × 16" (25 × 40.5 cm) swatches in your chosen colorway to test a larger area of your stencil design.

16 If satisfied with the color combination, cut out your garment or project in the same colors and complete as instructed.

Explore our color play in chapter 5: Practice, beginning on page 160.

ABOVE Fabric Swatch, Abstract in Camel, airbrushed using textile paint and ready for embroidery

OPPOSITE Fabric Swatch, Abstract in Camel, embroidered using Negative Reverse Appliqué technique with the Backstitch and Variegated Embroidery Floss

STENCIL MOTIF DESIGN 101

DRAFTING A STENCIL requires a brief understanding of the geometry of shapes and how to connect a stencil motif to the stencil material. Often this work requires "stencil bridges," as the bridges connect shapes to the stencil material.

MATERIALS

Inspiration

Pencil

Black pens and markers with different points, from fine to extra-wide

Tracing paper (large enough for your desired repeat)

Paper scissors

Gridded cutting mat

Photocopies or tracings of shapes

Photocopies in black-and-white of motif ideas

Tape

Butcher paper

Graph paper

Ruler

Curves (optional)

While there is no given method for producing a stencil design, here are some general steps to follow:

1 Gather inspiration.

2 Start with tracing or drawing shapes.

3 Color in shapes with a black marker to see if a shape requires bridges.

4 Cut out shapes and tape to butcher paper or trace shapes to create a collection of shapes to form a motif. Photocopies of shapes can be used in this step as well. Tape securely into place.

ABOVE The simple letter A at top left, when cut out on the perimeter, will also lose the island—the hollow, triangular center, known as a counter. The second A shows how the triangular island, or counter, is lost when cutting a stencil. The missing counter can be left out of of the finished stencil, or bridges can be added to hold it in place as part of the finished design. In the second row, there are three stencil variations of an A with built-in bridges to hold the triangular island in place or to create the illusion of an inner triangle.

When designing a stencil motif, you can plan for bridges or go back after the motif is finished and add bridges to make sure that your stencil design is robust. The wider the bridge, the stronger the stencil.

Instructions on previous and following pages are for creating a motif manually with pen and/ or photocopied shapes. Any of this work can also be accomplished on a computer program of your choice. All materials are optional. Choose the method that makes you happy; choose the materials that make you happy.

See chapter 5, Practice (pages 160–174), for more on stencils.

FOLLOWING Pennant Felt Facets stencil for appliqué; Mylar 21 Years Poem stencil

Stencils can be made from any material that can be cut and hold the stencil shape. Paint—or stencil method of choice—passes through the cut stencil opening and onto the fabric using a variety of techniques (see page 256 for information on transferring stencils).

5 Within the motif, experiment with line widths. Do you want a line that is thick or thin, constant or changing?

6 Within the motif, experiment with proportion, scale, spacing, and interval. Do you want shapes that are all similar or different, close together or farther apart?

7 Adjust the shapes as desired. Color in any shapes you suspect may need bridges.

8 Trace motif again to test pattern placement and bridges.

9 Color in shapes to examine positive/negative space.

10 Use tracing paper, a copy machine, or computer to reverse the positive/negative space. Examine relationships between individual shapes within the motif and adjust as needed.

11 When you are satisfied with your final motif, and if an allover pattern is desired, experiment with repeating motifs within grid structures.

12 For repeating patterns, you may decide to add or take away shapes from the motif—or alter the motif at the edges to fit together better in repetition.

13 Trace, photocopy, or use a computer to finalize the desired repeat.

It's important to remember that textile and surface design are learned by practice and may take years to master. After forty years, I'm still working to master this process.

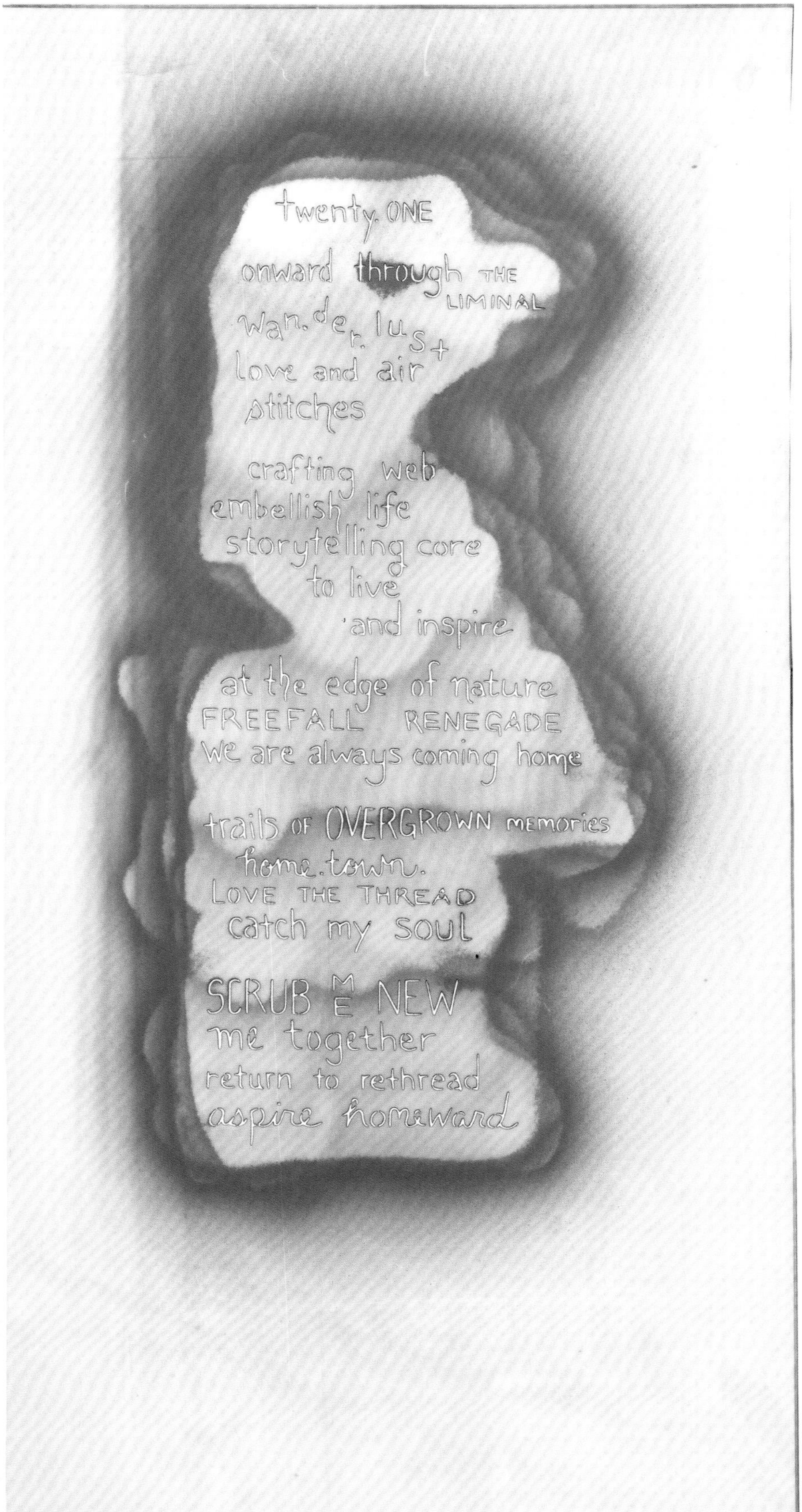

twenty ONE

onward through THE
LIMINAL
wan.der. lu.st
love and air
stitches

crafting web
embellish life
storytelling core
to live
and inspire

at the edge of nature
FREEFALL   RENEGADE
We are always coming home

trails of OVERGROWN memories
home.town.
LOVE THE THREAD
catch my soul

SCRUB M̃E NEW
me together
return to rethread
aspire homeward

STENCIL TRANSFER

STENCILS CAN BE MADE of any material, from paper to Mylar film. We've had projects that used pennant felt, an easy-to-cut material that holds up over many years, to posterboard for quick projects that don't require long use. Today, the majority of our stencils are cut from Mylar film. These stencils used in combination with one of the transfer materials that follow, are a quick and easy way to add a pattern in a single motif or repeat to a project, garment, or fabric.

Textile paint has long been our transfer method of choice. This robust and readily available material can be thickened to use for screen printing or diluted with water to create a watercolor-like effect. As of this writing, we are exploring ways to create our own transfer pigments from natural materials and dyes.

When mixing paints or pigments, work in small increments, adding a drop or two at a time, as even small amounts can change a color dramatically. Always test paint colors and transfer techniques on a fabric scrap before beginning a final project. Every batch of paint will be slightly different. For this reason, once you've decided on a final paint color or colors, mix enough to complete your final project—unless you desire a mottled effect of differing shades.

Some paints require heat to set and become permanently bonded to the fabric surface. Always read the manufacturer's instructions and test a painted swatch of your fabric of choice by washing. You may also choose to do a more robust wash test by washing multiple times to determine how a paint will react on fabric over time. This can be as simple as adding a swatch to every like-colored wash you run.

Similar to a sewing tool kit, we've built a kit of tools for accomplishing a wide variety of stencil transfer methods. Experiment with all the transfer methods that follow, for many different effects.

AIRBRUSH

The first time I used a stencil on fabric, I purchased cans of spray paint from the same hardware store I'd purchased the first needles and threads (see page 159). As the project grew in scale, we began using textile paints that were compatible with a simple hobby airbrush gun and a compressor—also purchased at the local hardware store.

PAINTBRUSH

Choose a range of brushes intended for water-based paints such as gouache. We keep both flat and round, wide and thin brushes in our kit for different effects. Clean brushes well after each use and they can be used for a lifetime.

SPONGE

Like spray bottles, sponges come in a wide range of options. Each type of sponge, from naturally grown to man-made varieties, creates a distinct texture. Makeup-type sponges are for a smooth coating of paint and can be used over and over again.

SPRAY BOTTLE

Spray bottles come in a wide range of sizes and options. Pump- and trigger-action bottles are available, and many common household cleaners come in bottles with adjustable nozzles. Some bottles work better than others and it is good work to test the options. With some nozzles, paint tends to spray inconsistently and can create splotches. If the character of splotchy paint is part of the design, this is a great tool. Play with mixtures of paint and water to get the effect you're looking to achieve. The more water you use, the more transparent the color will become.

TEXTILE OR PERMANENT MARKERS

An array of textile and permanent markers are available in a variety of colors and points. These tools are easy to use and often simple to make a permanent bond. Be sure to test all brands, types, and colors for wash durability before beginning any project.

ABOUT ALABAMA CHANIN AND THE SCHOOL OF MAKING

Alabama Chanin

The company that has become what Alabama Chanin is today began early in 2000 with the creation of hand-sewn garments made from cotton jersey T-shirts by founder and slow-design pioneer Natalie Chanin. We are a leader in elevated craft due to a strong belief in tradition and dedication to locally sewn garments and goods—both hand- and machine-sewn. We maintain responsible, ethical, and sustainable practices holding ourselves to the highest standards for quality. We are makers and educators, working to elevate and merge design, craft, and fashion. At Alabama Chanin, we preserve traditions of community, design, producing, and living arts by examining work and life through the acts of storytelling, photography, education, and making.

OPPOSITE Embroidered 21 Years Poem (see page 214 for the 21 Years Jacket)

The School of Making

The School of Making was officially founded in 2014 and is the educational arm of Alabama Chanin. Its goal is to incorporate the best of fashion, craft, and design under one roof, focusing on a responsible supply chain, including 100 percent organic materials, how-to books, workshops, and kits for garments and home furnishings.

A DIY collection of garment patterns and hand-sewn projects inspired from the Studio Book Series are launched on a regular basis.

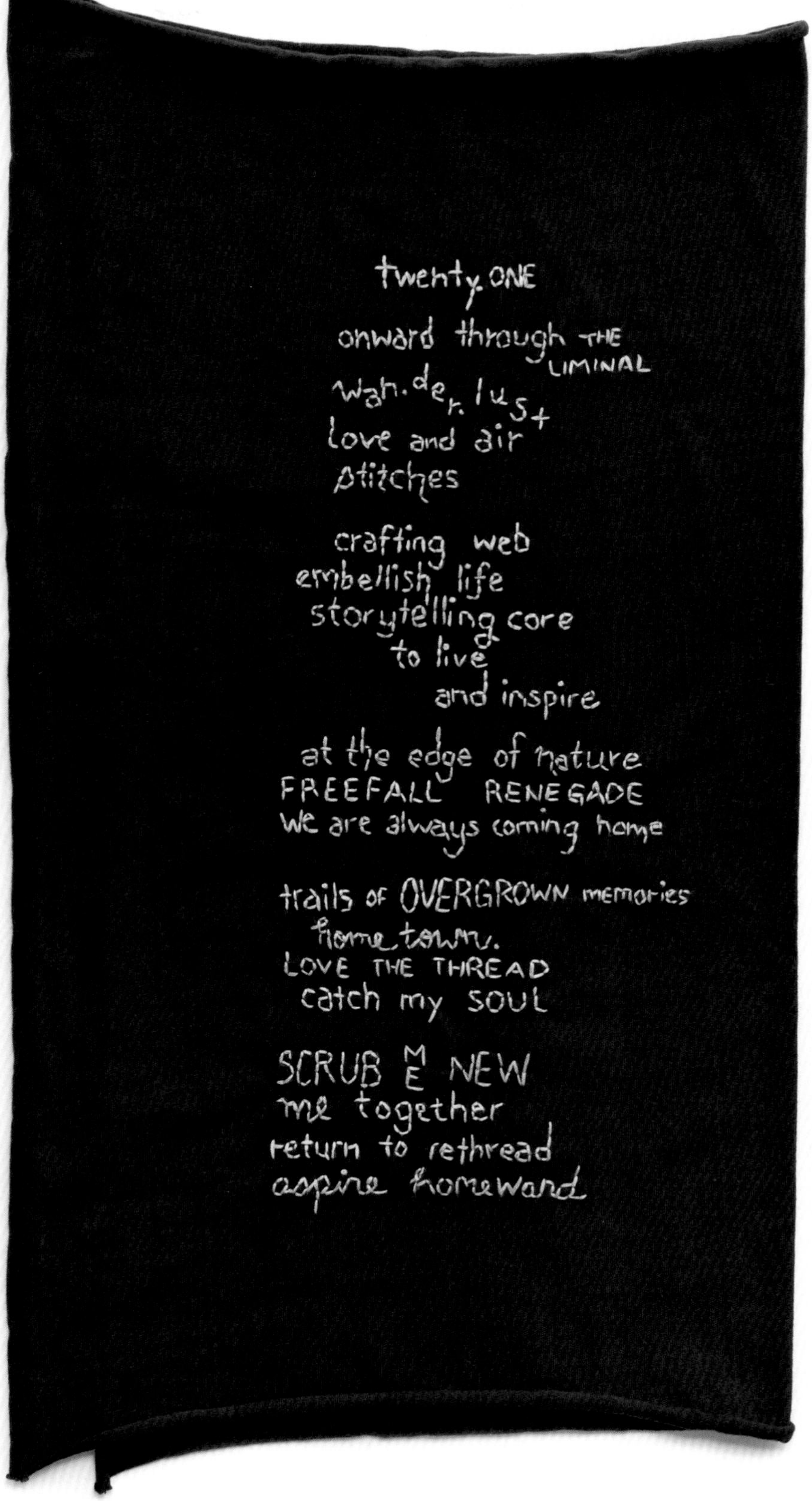

twenty.ONE

onward through THE
LIMINAL
wan.de.r.lust
love and air
stitches

crafting web
embellish life
storytelling core
to live
and inspire

at the edge of nature
FREEFALL   RENEGADE
we are always coming home

trails of OVERGROWN memories
home town.
LOVE THE THREAD
catch my SOUL

SCRUB ᴹᴱ NEW
me together
return to rethread
aspire homeward

ALABAMA STUDIO

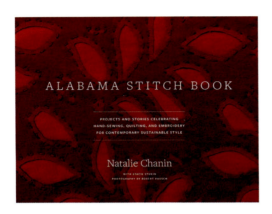

ALABAMA STITCH BOOK

This first book in the series focuses on recycled T-shirts as the basis for a collection of twenty projects. The book includes the Swing Skirt, Corset, and Shawl patterns, three beloved projects from The School of Making. Additionally, there are four stencil designs—Bloomers, Rose, Rooster, and Lace Stripe—plus Natalie's famous biscuit recipe and stories about cotton and community. *Alabama Stitch Book* received an updated cover and introduction in 2018, celebrating ten years in publication.

Alabama Studio Style followed *Alabama Stitch Book* in 2010 and was retired from print in 2019.

ALABAMA STUDIO SEWING + DESIGN

Alabama Studio Sewing + Design launched in 2012 as an encyclopedic compilation of appliqué and reverse appliqué variations, including sewing, stenciling, and fabric design techniques in the series. To celebrate ten years of publication in 2022, the book will be rereleased with an updated cover and introduction.

Paper patterns in the book include five basic garment styles—the T-shirt Top/Bolero, the Fitted Dress/Skirt/Tunic, each of which can be cut out and constructed in a variety of ways to create endless variation. Additionally, there are patterns and instructions for four accessories including the Poncho, Tied Wrap, Bucket Hat, and Fingerless Gloves, and eight stencils including Anna's Garden, June's Spring, Fern, Paisley, Kristina's Rose, Stars, Climbing Daisy, and Facets.

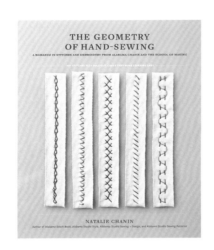

ALABAMA STUDIO SEWING PATTERNS

Alabama Studio Sewing Patterns, the fourth and last book in the Studio Book Series, published in 2015, is inspired by requests for a wider variety of garment patterns. The introduction allows that "some people want looser styles; some people want a wider selection of sleeves options; others want more sizes." Since it is impossible to make a collection of patterns to fit every body type, the book offers suggestions, tips, and instructions for altering patterns to suit individual preferences.

The book contains twenty-eight digital patterns and is full of directions for customizing these and all patterns for use with cotton jersey.

THE GEOMETRY OF HAND-SEWING

The Geometry of Hand-Sewing: A Romance in Stitches and Embroidery, the fifth book from Alabama Chanin and The School of Making, was published in 2017. This volume focuses on the stitches themselves rather than projects or garments. Embroidery stitches are broken down into simple geometric grid systems that make learning elaborate stitches a stitch-by-letter process. This breakthrough method is elaborated in more than one hundred stitches, with photos of both the front and back sides and guidelines for modifying stitches. Included are two plastic stitching cards, which can be removed from the book, with the grids for each stitch in the book.

INDEX OF PHOTO AND DESIGN CHOICES

TO DOCUMENT AND PRESERVE hand-sewn fabric designs and developments, Alabama Chanin has maintained a fabric library of 10 × 16-inch embroidery swatches for almost two decades. All of the fabric swatches included in this book are part of this living library.

All hand-embroidered fabrics and products at Alabama Chanin and The School of Making are given or assigned numbers which track information about fabrics, colors, details, and the artisans who've created each piece. What began with #00001 has reached #31423 at the time of publication of this book.

All fabrics and garments pictured are hand-embroidered from organic cotton jersey.

Appliqué | STITCH: Straight | TEXTILE PAINT: Slate | THREAD: Black | KNOTS: Inside | PHOTO: Abraham Rowe

PAGE 56-57: Graffiti Tee | Alabama Chanin | PHOTO: Rinne Allen

PAGE 59: Muscle Shoals Sound Studio | PHOTO: Robert Rausch

PAGE 60: City of Muscle Shoals, Alabama, "Hit Recording Capital of the World" | PHOTO: Robert Rausch

PAGE 61: Organic cotton seedlings, Northwest Alabama | PHOTO: Erin Dailey

PAGE 61: Sewing machine detail in Building 14 | PHOTO: Rinne Allen

PAGE 62: Mick Jagger recording at Muscle Shoals Sound Studio | PHOTO: David Hood

PAGE 62: Muscle Shoals Sound Studio T-shirt | PHOTO: Robert Rausch

PAGE 63: Muscle Shoals Sound Studio, Sheffield, Alabama | PHOTO: Robert Rausch

PAGE 64-65: Fabric Swatch #26674 | Alabama Chanin | PHOTO: Abraham Rowe

PAGE 66: Fabric Swatch #29495 | Alabama Chanin | PHOTO: Robert Rausch

PAGE 68-69: Fabric Swatch #29980 | Alabama Chanin | PHOTO: Robert Rausch

PAGE 71: Detail of hand-sewn label | Alabama Chanin | PHOTO: Rinne Allen

PAGE 72: Field at Mooresville, Limestone County, Alabama, Muscle Shoals National Heritage Area, Hidden Spaces project | PHOTO: Abraham Rowe

PAGE 74: Piney Creek, Tennessee River backwater, Limestone County, Alabama, Muscle Shoals National Heritage Area, Hidden Spaces project | PHOTO: Abraham Rowe

PAGE 75: Spiral screen for fabric printing | Alabama Chanin | PHOTO: Robert Rausch

PAGE 75: County Road, Limestone County, Alabama, Muscle Shoals National Heritage Area, Hidden Spaces Project | PHOTO: Abraham Rowe

PAGE 76-77: Fabric Swatch #22297 | Alabama Chanin | PHOTO: Abraham Rowe

PAGE 78: Koger Island, Muscle Shoals National Heritage Area, Hidden Spaces project | PHOTO: Abraham Rowe

PAGE 79: Lovelace Crossroads production office | PHOTO: Robert Rausch

PAGE 79: Between fields in Lauderdale County, Alabama | PHOTO: Robert Rausch

PAGE 81: "December Sky," Lovelace Crossroads | PHOTO: Natalie Chanin

PAGE 83: "Sister Shirt" | Alabama Collection | PHOTO: Natalie Chanin

PAGE 84-85: Spreads from *Sioseh 17: Alabama* | Photos: Sissi Farassat

PAGE 87: The Original *Stitch* VHS cassette | PHOTO: Robert Rausch

PAGE 88: Machine-Appliquéd Vintage T-Shirt | Alabama Collection | PHOTO: Robert Rausch

PAGE 90: Instructions from the original Stitch Book | Alabama Collection | PHOTO: Robert Rausch

PAGE 92-93: Fabric Swatch #27943 | The School of Making | FABRIC WEIGHT: Medium | FABRIC OUTER LAYER: Mud | FABRIC BACKING LAYER: Blalck | STENCIL: Bloomers | TECHNIQUE: Reverse

ABOUT THE AUTHOR

NATALIE "ALABAMA" CHANIN is the owner and designer of Alabama Chanin. She has a degree in environmental design with a focus on industrial and craft-based textiles from North Carolina State University. Natalie has worked as a fashion design, stylist, and costume designer; in 2000, she returned to her home to begin the sustainable work that has become Alabama Chanin.

Since 2000, Alabama Chanin has expanded to include a family of businesses: the Alabama Chanin collection, The School of Making, and Building 14 Design + Manufacturing Services. All facets work together to create a collaborative community and idea exchange, healthy growth, and a love of quality goods that last. Chanin continues to design and to lecture on craft traditions—using conversations to bridge generational, economic, and cultural gaps. She has written six books and is a mother of two, an avid gardener, and an enthusiastic cook and entertainer from her home in Florence, Alabama.

ACKNOWLEDGMENTS

Thank you.

The Alabama Chanin artisans and team members who have been there across time and space. Without the deep talent, ceaseless commitment, and sense of humor, this work would never have been possible. I'm grateful to one and all—past, present, and future.

All of our guests of Alabama Chanin and The School of Making who have entrusted us with their wardrobes, workshops, dinners, weekends, and thousands of adventures along the way.

Shawna Mullen, who encouraged me to proceed with this work through many complications, delays, Covid-19, and, as the great writer, teacher, and humorist Anne Lamott might whisper, some "shitty first drafts." Editors make all the difference in the world.

Abrams, the publisher of this book and many of the most beautiful books I own in my massive and growing library. I'm grateful for accepted delays, and format changes, and that they have believed in this work across a collection of, now, six books.

Ansley Quiros, my wise, beautiful, thoughtful friend, neighbor, and fellow walker, fellow traveler, and collaborator. This book is a better read because of Ansley's whip-smart intellect, deep understanding of the history of all things, and kind way of always telling the truth. She is a treasure.

My mother, Myra Brown, the brilliant math-ematician, lover of geometry, knitter, maker, and traveler, who, during the process of writing this book, slipped into dementia and Alzheimer's disease and, in many ways, showed me a new understanding of life. And to Jim Brown, who is by her side.

Thank you to the Alzheimer's Foundation of America—who helped me see that life, and end of life, *can be lived* with honesty, honor, and humor. You never understand the important work of this organization until you need the organization. Their twenty-four-hour helpline number: (866) 232-8484.

And an enormous thank-you to my Al-Anon friends and family—you helped (and are still helping) me learn *how to live* with honesty, honor, and humor. Keep showing up.

To Zach and Maggie Chanin, my children and my heart. It's never easy, always full. I love you both to the moon and back again. (And again.)

And to Stella Ruth Chanin, who keeps me laughing, dreaming, designing, and making biscuits. I love you, my sweet, designing granddaughter. May all your drawings come true.

To Billy and Sherry Smith: none of this without you.

To the Kitchen Sisters, Catherine Burns, and The Moth. Thank you for listening, teaching, and giving so much.

I'm so eternally grateful to Nelly, the people of Venezuela, and all the travelers who shared my time in Los Roques and across Venezuela—and yes, grateful for birds and barracuda too.

To Tim Buie for conversations about color, design, and vocabulary—forever fascinating.

These people have touched my life in the most wonderful ways, making this work possible: Rinne Allen, Cathy Bailey, Carrie Barske-Crawford, Rosanne Cash, Chandra Cox, Erin Dailey, Goode and Brad Dethero, John T. Edge, Melanie Falick, Sissi Farassat, Lisa Fox, Barbara Frasier, Kay Gardiner, Jakob Glatz, Paul Graves, Diane Hall, Carol and Paul Jiganti, Charles Joyner, Maira Kalman, Enrico Marone-Cinzano, Birgit Mitterbauer, Angie Mosier, Bonnie Mudler, Igor Orovac, Sun Young Park, Michael Pause, Elaine and Buddy Poorman, Jennifer Rausch, Erin Reitz, Steven Smith, Gael Towey, Jess Turner, Eva Whitechapel, and Judith Winfrey.

Editor: Shawna Mullen
Designer: Sarah Gifford
Design Manager: Danny Maloney
Managing Editor: Lisa Silverman
Production Manager: Kathleen Gaffney

Library of Congress Control Number:
2022932895

ISBN: 978-1-4197-5277-3
eISBN: 978-1-64700-218-3

Printed and bound in China
10 9 8 7 6 5 4 3 2 1

Abrams books are available at special discounts when
purchased in quantity for premiums and promotions as
well as fundraising or educational use. Special editions
can also be created to specification. For details, contact
specialsales@abramsbooks.com or the address below.

Abrams® is a registered trademark of
Harry N. Abrams, Inc.

ABRAMS
The Art of Books

195 Broadway
New York, NY 10007
abramsbooks.com

To document and preserve hand-sewn fabric designs
and developments, Alabama Chanin has maintained
a fabric library of 10 × 16-inch embroidery swatches
for almost two decades. All of the fabric swatches
included in this book are part of this living library.

Unless otherwise noted, all fabrics pictured are
hand-embroidered from organic cotton jersey.

PAGE 1 Fabric swatch, Dots in Sapphire Blue,
hand-painted, Alabama Chanin

PAGE 2 Fabric swatch, Spirals in Blue Slate, appliqué,
The School of Making

PAGES 4-5 Detail of Natalie's backyard garden,
including her Purple Martin Gourd Houses. Plant
life and nature inspire much of the design work for
Alabama Chanin and The School of Making (see Tiny
Eggs fabric on page 28, fabric design inspired by
Purple Martin Gourds).

PAGE 6 Fabric swatch, Abstract in Verdant Green
and Natural, reverse appliqué, The School of Making
(explore a variety of Abstract color and design
variations in chapter 5, beginning on page 160)

PAGES 8-9 "The Nap," featuring a collection of
garments and the Anna's Garden design in reverse
and negative reverse appliqué, Alabama Chanin

PAGE 10 Fabric swatch, Abstract in Navy Blue, reverse
appliqué, The School of Making